I
RESPECTFULLY
DISAGREE

I
RESPECTFULLY
DISAGREE

How to Have **Difficult Conversations** in a **Divided World**

Justin Jones-Fosu

Berrett–Koehler Publishers, Inc.

Berrett-Koehler Publishers, Inc.
1333 Broadway, Suite 1000
Oakland, CA 94612-1921
Tel: (510) 817-2277
Fax: (510) 817-2278
www.bkconnection.com

ORDERING INFORMATION

Quantity sales. Special discounts are available on quantity purchases by corporations,
associations, and others. For details, contact the "Special Sales Department" at the
Berrett-Koehler address above.

Individual sales. Berrett-Koehler publications are available through most bookstores. They
can also be ordered directly from Berrett-Koehler: Tel: (800) 929-2929; Fax: (802) 864-7626;
www.bkconnection.com.

Orders for college textbook / course adoption use. Please contact Berrett-Koehler:
Tel: (800) 929-2929; Fax: (802) 864-7626.

Distributed to the U.S. trade and internationally by Penguin Random House Publisher
Services.

Berrett-Koehler and the BK logo are registered trademarks of Berrett-Koehler Publishers, Inc.

Printed in the United States of America.

Berrett-Koehler books are printed on long-lasting acid-free paper. When it is available,
we choose paper that has been manufactured by environmentally responsible processes.
These may include using trees grown in sustainable forests, incorporating recycled paper,
minimizing chlorine in bleaching, or recycling the energy produced at the paper mill.

Library of Congress Cataloging-in-Publication Data

Names: Jones-Fosu, Justin, author.
Title: I respectfully disagree : how to have difficult conversations in a
  divided world / Justin Jones-Fosu.
Description: First edition. | Oakland, CA : Berrett-Koehler Publishers,
  Inc., [2024] | Includes bibliographical references and index.
Identifiers: LCCN 2023045214 (print) | LCCN 2023045215 (ebook) | ISBN
  9781523006519 (paperback) | ISBN 9781523006526 (pdf) | ISBN
  9781523006533 (epub)
Subjects: LCSH: Interpersonal communication. | Interpersonal relations. |
  Communication—Psychological aspects.
Classification: LCC BF637.C45 J69 2024 (print) | LCC BF637.C45 (ebook) |
  DDC 153.6—dc23/eng/20231226
LC record available at https://lccn.loc.gov/2023045214
LC ebook record available at https://lccn.loc.gov/2023045215

First Edition

31 30 29 28 27 26 25 24 10 9 8 7 6 5 4 3 2 1

Book producer and text designer: Happenstance Type-O-Rama
Cover designer: David Ter-Avanesyan
Photographs and illustrations: Justin Jones-Fosu

To my bride, Tanya, you have made me a better person with your calming love, radiant joy, and respectful disagreements. I pray that we continue to uplift each other, challenge each other, and learn from each other. One thing that I will always respectfully agree about . . . you are my dream come true!

To the fantastic four, my amazing kiddos tribe: Isaiah, Lydia, Peter, and David . . . WOW! I have seen A LOT of disagreements and not all of them respectful (I have some work to do), but I have noticed your genuine love for each other, for me, and for humanity. Knowing that you are inheriting this world makes me breathe a little easier!

CONTENTS

INTRODUCTION: The Problem, the Solution, and the Tortoise   1

PART I: What Are the Divides? The Challenge to Respectfully Disagree

CHAPTER 1: Three Stories and a Why: *Why Should You Respectfully Disagree, Anyway?*   19

CHAPTER 2: Why I Respectfully Disagree with Aretha Franklin: *The Choice of Golden Respect*   33

CHAPTER 3: A Picture of the Past: *A Catalyst for Who You Are Today*   53

CHAPTER 4: The Disagreement Divide: *Are You Building Up Barriers or Bridging the Divide?*   67

PART II: The 5 Pillars of Bridging the Divide

CHAPTER 5: How You See Is What You Get: *Pillar 1, Challenge Your Perspective*   87

CHAPTER 6: The Teacher Appears When the Student Is Ready: *Pillar 2, Be the Student*   113

CHAPTER 7: Don't Take the Exit on People: *Pillar 3, Cultivate Your Curiosity*   129

CHAPTER 8: Fifty Shades of . . . : *Pillar 4, Seek the Gray*   145

CHAPTER 9: A Path Forward:
Pillar 5, Agree to Respect   161

CHAPTER 10: What Do I Do Now?
A Call to Meaningful Action   181

NOTES   187

RESOURCES   197

ACKNOWLEDGMENTS   211

INDEX   215

ABOUT THE AUTHOR   227

INTRODUCTION

The Problem, the Solution, and the Tortoise

Have you heard these phrases lately?

"You're wrong."

"How could you believe that?"

"Anyone with intelligence would never think that."

"Why would you vote for that person?"

"I think that's just stupid."

"The [political group] is the biggest threat to our country."

"Those people are just wrong!"

"We need to take back our country."

"How could they ever come to that conclusion?"

"Those people don't use their brains—they just follow blindly!"

The fact that you've probably heard these phrases or a variation of them speaks to a continued and growing problem in the world today: how divided people are on the big topics of politics, race, immigration, and so many others. It also speaks to how divided we are on topics such as what movie is the best, who is the best golfer of all time, and why all bald men are so handsome (there is no debate on that one . . . ha!). The truth is that we're not just divided but also growing more and more disrespectful toward each other, and it doesn't have to be that way.

WHAT'S THE PROBLEM?

Have you noticed that we live in a time of extreme polarization on many fronts? Some might even argue that we are beyond polarization and are now into outright hostility and violence. Pew Research Center's findings sketch a bleak image: an increasing number of people in the United States view those on the opposite political side as lazy, immoral, closed-minded, dishonest, and unintelligent.[1] This toxic assumption gnaws away at our common ground, deepening the abyss of misunderstanding. It's a global concern, no longer confined within the borders of any one nation. Not only are we facing hostilities between political parties globally, but we are also facing serious disagreements that are negatively impacting people's lives and worse.

Consider the grim report card from the United Nations, which provides a stark revelation about our global community's state.[2] Thousands of innocent lives have been lost in the world's most gruesome conflicts, with civilians—women and children—often paying the heaviest price. These aren't mere numbers; they're echoes of shattered homes, dreams turned to dust, and the tragic human toll our inability to bridge our differences incurs.

An astounding 25 percent of the world's population dwells in regions scarred by serious conflicts. Visualize this: every fourth person you encounter potentially bears invisible wounds of a conflict they never wished for. And this trauma isn't confined to the distant past—in recent years, over 80 million individuals were compelled to abandon their homes due to conflict, violence, and human rights abuses.[3] Again, these aren't just numbers; they're a deafening plea for us to rise, to evolve, to be better.

What's also baffling is that small pockets of people want to create conflict so that they can have power over others, and they are willing to do anything it takes to sow seeds of discord to pit person against person and group against group. However, we're not powerless in the face of all of this. The work of respectful disagreement is one strategy of many to deflate the attacks against our dehumanization and the dehumanization of others. We have lost touch (if we ever had it) with the humanity in each other. We continue to see each other as objects to be overtaken and not people to be valued and respected.

One resounding issue is people who agree to disagree but still do it disrespectfully. Respectful disagreement is not about saying all the right things, but rather speaking from the right heart!

The Focus of This Book

This book is certainly not making the claim that respect alone can solve the world's biggest problems. But respect on an interpersonal level, in our day-to-day lives, can plant seeds of change in the hearts of those we encounter. Yes, there are many global examples of disrespectfully disagreeing, but I want to focus on the issues that you face directly with others at home, on your team, at work, and in your communities.

We have dehumanized each other through the process of labeling and generalizing and by forgetting that just because someone does or believes X doesn't mean that they do or believe Y. In doing so, we have lost the chance to discover and to let people surprise us, and the sad truth is that people might be looking at us with the same labels and generalizations. So why should we aspire to humanize others? There's an urgent need for respect, understanding, and empathy that transcends our personal space and permeates the global sphere—because beneath the facades of our political affiliations, beneath our multicolored cultures and varied beliefs, we are all fundamentally human. Our collective survival and advancement hinge on acknowledging this shared humanity and nurturing our ability for compassion, respectful disagreement, and constructive dialogue.

Our homes yearn for this spirit as we navigate intricate conversations with our family, roommates, and yes, even for some of us, our pets (a fascinating discussion for another day). Our workplaces stand to gain immeasurably from it. In a study on conversational receptiveness, the researchers concluded, "Employees who feel that their boss listens to them experience less emotional exhaustion and report being more willing to stay in their positions; and open-mindedness between supervisors and employees leads to more effective resolutions to workplace conflict."[4]

Although we often believe we excel at making others feel acknowledged, research exposes an uncomfortable reality: people routinely overestimate their ability to ensure others feel heard. The researchers go on to state, "In other words, balanced and thoughtful consideration of opposing perspectives is the exception rather than the rule."

We need to pivot from erecting walls to constructing bridges, from sowing discord to nurturing connections. It's in our capacity to listen, empathize, and comprehend that we find the roadmap to a more harmonious, inclusive world. If nothing else, we find a more peaceful existence for us as individuals. I have witnessed behaviors by adults, in media and real life, that would warrant a disciplinary action if exhibited by my children. We can—and must—do better.

THE SOLUTION

Picture a world where you can express your dissent without fear of the ensuing emotional whirlwind or the specter of division. Visualize a conversation where you feel heard, respected, and valued, even when you stand on the opposing side of the argument. Imagine an atmosphere where you can vehemently disagree with someone yet fiercely uphold their humanity simultaneously. Isn't that a thrilling, even slightly heady, proposition?

Consider this book your passport to a new realm. It's an anthem for fostering understanding, acceptance, and respectful disagreement in a world all too often carved up by conflicting views. But let's set our expectations right. This book is not some enchanting potion conjuring an immediate wonderland of universal consensus. Rather, it's a compass, a handbook for cultivating our capacity to differ without diminishing others or our own dignity. This book is not about bathing in feel-good sentiments or spreading generic love. It's a pragmatic guide, geared to help you recognize each other's humanity, even when every fiber of your being resists.

Yes, there's a wealth of remarkable books out there on conflict resolution and efficient handling of disagreements. I am honored to contribute to this collective wisdom. This book aims to distinguish itself by its accessibility and relevance to everyday life. It's crafted to help us lean into the people we meet at home, at work, in our communities (and, yes, even online), affecting all facets of our existence.

We often restrain our true thoughts, fearing we might stoke the embers of discord or sever precious bonds. But what if we could stay true to ourselves, express our views in their entirety, and still preserve the bond of respect? That's the learning this book seeks to impart. It's more than a skill—it's a mindset, a life philosophy we should all aspire to embody.

Why Me?

So why me, and what has motivated me to tackle this challenging topic? I grew up in Grand Rapids, Michigan (holds up hand to show you where), and initially my family struggled financially. We were a household of a single mom (my hero) and two very challenging little boys. One thing we never struggled with was our mom's genuine love for us and willingness to engage difference. Not only did we attend different cultural festivals and bring exchange students from around the world into our home, but my mom made sure we intentionally experienced things we disagreed with. We attended events centered on spiritual beliefs and practices that differed from our own, and we sometimes listened to speakers with different political beliefs than those we shared as a family.

These experiences shaped me but also made me a bit odd. I was a nerd initially living in the hood (a story for another day). Even though we faced initial financial hardship, my mom-e (as I affectionately call her) made sure we studied and took education very seriously. I would walk to and from elementary school ferociously reading the latest John Grisham and Stephen Covey books. Unfortunately, I also talked differently than my peers and was constantly called "white boy"! I quickly learned that I wasn't Black enough for the Black kids and I wasn't white enough for the white kids. This feeling of not fitting in permeated my adolescent growth all the way into college, where I was somewhat popular but never really in one group. I just didn't fit in.

It wasn't until I attended a diversity and inclusion session during an internship in Louisiana that it finally hit me why. Sitting in the middle of the U-shaped classroom, I quickly put my hands to my face to catch the overwhelming flood of tears that had drenched it. I concluded that I wasn't *supposed* to fit in, because I was meant to be a bridge between others. I would come to learn that this wasn't just about race but about many more complexities in life. The seeds of bridging the divide that my mother planted were beginning to sprout, and I was on a mission to help others become bridges, too!

This led me to start a company that is now called Work. Meaningful., and one area of our research is what we call the *Inclusive Mindset*. Over two decades of helping organizations and leaders create more inclusive cultures, I came to realize this book was necessary. In every Inclusive Mindset learning experience, I would explain that inclusion is not just about race, gender, and identity but that it impacts all of us and is about all of us! It isn't a kumbaya experience where we all hold hands and sing in unison with closed eyes U-N-I-T-Y (thanks, Queen Latifah). My next statements formed the basis of my future research and learning experiences: "Real inclusion is not that we will always agree, but will we still choose to respect each other when we disagree? We can vehemently disagree with someone's ideology and still passionately pursue their humanity!"

This has grown into an area of focus for our company as my colleagues and I have worked with Fortune 50 companies, universities, and youth to help them embody the Inclusive Mindset, experiences that led me to write *The Inclusive Mindset: How to Cultivate Diversity in Your Everyday Life*.[5] This work is embodied in what we believe the world can be, and we are working toward that aim in what we call the *Inclusive Mindset Vision*. This vision comes from the desire to improve our humanhood and create a world that works for all (thanks, Berrett-Koehler). This vision is aspirational, and it's one that I challenge myself to grow in each and every day.

Can you envision this world with me?

The Inclusive Mindset Vision

The world can be a place where . . .

- People are treated with value, dignity, and respect with full regard of what they look like, how they identify, and what they believe.

- People engage others every day with a sense of wonderment and curiosity.

- People disagree respectfully while honoring the perspectives of others.

- Everyone feels included, seen, and heard, and the voices of the marginalized are elevated and amplified.

- People stand up for others when they see injustice occurring and challenge systems that don't work for others.

- People don't have to be perfect and can receive grace as they learn from their mistakes.

- Diversity and inclusion are no longer an initiative but part of our everyday lives, and no longer a mandate but simply a mindset.

This is the world we believe in. This is what we believe the world can be.

This vision is important to this book because it points directly to the humanity of us all, and respectfully disagreeing is one way to enforce that humanity. In our efforts to create a kinder, more empathetic world, having an Inclusive Mindset is a great first step, which starts with being inspired (heart), being prepared (head), and being encouraged to act (hand).

The Heart. Head. Hand. Model

One thing that became apparent to the people working with me toward this vision is that it often matters how topics are approached, which inspired the company to adopt the Heart. Head. Hand. Model as a way of learning and doing. Whereas most times efforts start with the head (knowledge), we have realized that long-lasting transformation must start from the heart (connection to the topic). Then we can access the hand (practical tools) to be able to go out and enact positive growth in our everyday lives—not so fast that we never have sustainable growth and never move the needle, but not so slow that we take for granted the challenges that many are facing in our global society.

I encourage you to see this book as a way to walk through this model as well. This is not simply a "how to" (head and hand) guide; it's a "why to" (heart) book designed to stir up your soul for goodness. While it is full of research, it is also full of relatable stories (both real and slightly fictionalized to protect identities) to help you apply this in your everyday life. This is where the approach of the tortoise comes in.

The Tortoise Principle

This book doesn't promise to be the magic remedy to all conflicts. Instead, I adopt an approach from my Inclusive Mindset work known as the Tortoise Principle, inspired by my favorite childhood fable, "The Tortoise and the Hare." In the fable, a proud and speedy hare brags about how fast he is, mocking the slow-moving tortoise. To prove his superiority, the hare challenges the tortoise to a race. Confident of his win, the hare dashes forward and, seeing how far ahead he is, decides to take a nap midrace. The tortoise, however, remains steady and persistent. While the hare sleeps, the tortoise plods on and ultimately crosses the finish line first. When the hare awakens, he realizes his mistake too late. The tale serves as a timeless reminder that strategic and steady wins the race and underscores the values of persistence and humility.

For years, I've argued that we've misinterpreted this tale. We've labeled the tortoise as slow. But wasn't it rather strategic, advancing with purpose and consistency? It's only compared to the hare that the tortoise appears slow—and yet who claimed the victory in the end? Reading this book won't eradicate all your disrespectful disagreements (as I also still fall prey), but it will help you apply small bits of work every day, rather than a whirlwind makeover that won't last. After all, you've made positive change before.

Reflect on a time when you conquered a particularly tough challenge because you knew it would lead to better things. You pushed through the mistakes, challenges, and hurdles of life. You've accomplished this before, and you can do it again when the pressure mounts. You can be the catalyst the world needs, and more specifically, the catalyst the world you interact with every day needs for more respectful disagreement. Your growth and small acts of respect can have ripple effects you might never have imagined.

WHAT THIS BOOK IS AND IS NOT

I share this book not as an expert who navigates disagreements impeccably every time (in fact, I had a few disrespectful disagreements as I was researching and writing this), but as a fellow traveler on the journey toward more humane interactions and a commitment to uplift those I encounter. This is about cultivating a habit.

This journey won't be devoid of fun. I've laughed (and shed tears) multiple times while crafting this book. If you allow it to be, this book will transform you in similar ways it has transformed me.

You might think this book will guide you on convincing the "other" about the rightness of your perspective. Allow me to apologize up front—this isn't that book. Although I do share research on approaches that sometimes lead to shifts in perspective, the focus here is better understanding and humanizing the people around us. It's about honoring their worth in small ways every day.

In chapter 2, we delve deeper into what I call *Golden Respect* and how it deviates from societal norms. Simply put, Golden Respect acknowledges that every person on this planet (and even those floating in space) is inherently worthy and deserves to be treated as such. *Every person* has something valuable to contribute, and when we respect and humanize others, it enriches our learning. This leads to deeper understanding and awareness of ourselves and others and fewer assumptions about what we think others mean. Respecting others doesn't necessitate agreement, nor does it mean we "honor" them blindly, but it does entail recognizing their value and worth, even amidst major disagreements.

During my team's Inclusive Mindset workshops, we've always emphasized that we could vehemently disagree with someone's ideology yet fervently uphold their humanity. This perspective often resonates with the audience, and many requested deeper insights, identifying it as a crucial aspect to address. We began hosting learning experiences on the art of respectful disagreement not just to perform better but to be better humans. This book is the answer to our participants' desire to practically lean into the statement that respectful disagreement isn't about endorsing someone's ideology but about recognizing their humanity.

All Levels Welcome

You don't need to be a diplomat, conflict mediator, or negotiation expert to learn from this book. Truthfully, I didn't write this book for the experts, but rather for the everyday person in everyday life who wants to treat people a little better in their challenging conversations. The book's insights extend to anyone who has felt the sting of being misunderstood, sidelined, or even demonized because of their beliefs. It's also for you if you, like me, have done this to others. If you've wrestled with expressing your dissent without feeling a twinge of guilt or anxiety, then this book is your ally.

Together, we'll embark on a thrilling journey of professional growth, self-improvement, and mutual understanding. We'll learn to perceive disagreement not as a chasm of division but as a catalyst to build bridges of understanding, an invitation to humanize and empathize.

Now, imagine this: What if you approached every individual you meet like a member of your family, irrespective of their perspectives, convictions, or background? Now, some of you are reading this and saying, "Justin, have you met my family?!" I get it—family can be complicated, tricky, and very nuanced. When I discuss family, I talk about the good ones where, even though there are some members who are "out there," the family still comes together. It's one of the lessons I learned when living in Mississippi: the importance of family sticking together! Think of the transformative power in treating everyone with the same respect, dignity, and regard you'd accord to your own good kin, even amidst dissent or the throes of conflict.

If your default modus operandi involves yelling, name-calling, and flinging insults rather than engaging in respectful disagreement, I still encourage you to read on. You might discover an alternative by exploring how to break the habit of labeling and categorizing others, which will lead to more fulfilling personal and professional relationships.

At times, the clamor around us can convince us that respectful disagreements are a thing of the past, an unreachable ideal. Some might even suggest that we've crossed the point of no return based on the constant negativity of the news, with its sensational stories designed to keep us watching and, in some cases, hating each other. But I am here to assure you that as long as there are people, there is always a way forward. This book isn't just about navigating those high-stakes disagreements; it's about the day-to-day differences, too. Opinions about movies, decisions on projects, debates about what's for dinner—these are all part of the journey. Furthermore, this book gives you the foundation to grapple with the disagreement heavyweight topics: politics, religion, policing, and diversity/inclusion in our global society. Whether you are dealing with your children, your spouse, your neighbor, your co-worker, or your employees, this book will set the stage for you to be a better conversational partner.

Format, Flow, and Focus of the Book

Each chapter contains the following elements: (1) an illustration to introduce the chapter, (2) a relevant quote, (3) relevant stories, (4) an explanation and information about the topic of that chapter, and (5) Reflections and Actions.

In this book, I delve into the heart of the matter and introduce powerful tools that can help you more consistently and respectfully disagree with others you currently know and those you will meet. I'll unveil the 3Self Model, which helps you identify whether you're operating from a place of superiority, equality, or inferiority during disagreements. I'll guide you on how to construct fewer barriers and build more bridges in everyday disagreements. The foundation of this book lies in the 5 Pillars of Bridging the Divide. In part II, I'll decode these pillars and how they can be infused into your daily life.

If you're ready to dive deeper into more respectful disagreements, join me in chapter 1! See you there.

REFLECTIONS AND ACTIONS

1. What is one reason you chose to read this book?

2. Which line of the Inclusive Mindset Vision resonates the most with you and why?

3. What is one way you can apply the Tortoise Principle (strategic growth) in your everyday life?

PART I

What Are the Divides?

The Challenge to Respectfully Disagree

I don't have to agree with
you to like you or respect you.
—ANTHONY BOURDAIN

Chapter 1 focuses on connecting to the heart of the problem of respectfully disagreeing by providing multiple real-life scenarios of where we go wrong in disagreements. In chapter 2, we focus on redefining respect to what I call Golden Respect and explore the powerful choice we have to give it to others. We then dive into our past with chapter 3, as we focus on identifying how our past experiences, hurts, and family patterns shape how we disagree with others and hinder us from getting to Golden Respect. Lastly, chapter 4 introduces the 5 Pillars and identifies ways for us to bridge the divide instead of building up barriers.

The foundation of this part of the book is my Four Responses of Conversation Conflict model, shown in figure 1. This model illustrates the intersection of agreement/disagreement and respect/disrespect to help you understand

The Four Responses of Conversation Conflict

AGREEMENT

Disrespectful Agreement
Agrees publicly but privately disagrees, dishonest with self and/or others

Disrespectful Agreement

Respectful Agreement

Respectful Agreement
True alignment on the stated ideology or issue (Not our focus)

DISRESPECTFUL ←→ RESPECTFUL

Disrespectful Disagreement
Disagrees with contention and often dehumanizes others

Disrespectful Disagreement

Respectful Disagreement

Respectful Disagreement
The GOAL: Disagrees while humanizing others and self

DISAGREEMENT

FIGURE 1: The Four Responses of Conversation Conflict

the four responses we give based on conversation conflict. While respectful agreement is an outcome, it won't be the focus of the book. Instead, we'll focus on helping transition disrespectful disagreement and disrespectful agreement into more respectful disagreements.

CHAPTER 1

Three Stories and a Why

*Why Should You Respectfully
Disagree, Anyway?*

I n this chapter you will encounter a succession of stories
that are based on real-life conversations, interviews, and
situations my team has uncovered in our learning experiences, but some items have been changed to protect the
identities of those involved. If you skipped the Introduction,
consider going back and reading it, as it sets the tone for how
to engage with the book and the premise of more respectful
disagreements. Read these stories and identify if you relate to
any aspects in your personal or professional life.

JEN, ALISHA, AND A MOVIE

In the hushed quiet of the evening, Jen picked up the phone.
It was Alisha, her confidant, her ally, a woman who shared
the same passion for literature, parenting, and undiscovered
nooks of the world. They had met in a prestigious leadership
program in their city, a chance meeting that had bloomed into

an irreplaceable friendship. Their unique friendship grew to the highly critical thinking of critiquing independent films while consuming gourmet popcorn.

Alisha had recommended a film to Jen, a movie that she swore was a testament to cinematic excellence. She'd waited with bated breath for Jen's review, confident that her friend would love the film as deeply as she did.

However, Alisha's expectations came crashing down when she heard Jen's words. The movie wasn't great, Jen said. The storyline lacked coherence, and she struggled to see why Alisha would enjoy such a disorganized plot. Alisha felt a sting of insult, a rising defensiveness. Without thinking, she interrupted Jen, suggesting that her poor impression of the film was due to a bad day. She even lied, saying that four other friends adored the movie, and that it was highly rated on Rotten Tomatoes, though she hadn't verified that herself.

Jen internalized this and remembered her childhood, when she was forced to comply and not given a chance to express her independent thoughts. Jen's feelings were transported back to that little girl growing up in a household full of control and judgment. Jen snapped back, saying that even highly rated films could be disappointing. Jen wondered to herself why Alisha was taking this so seriously. After all, she thought, it was just a movie and didn't warrant the type of response Alisha was giving her.

Alisha, her voice raised, accused Jen of missing the beginning of the movie, something Jen was known to do often. She just couldn't believe that Jen had watched it entirely. If she had, Alisha was sure, Jen would've loved it. But Jen was firm—she had watched the entire film. However, Alisha refused to believe her.

Finally, with a forced calmness, Alisha—wanting to avoid further conflict at all costs due to her exhaustion from a marriage suffocated with it—suggested that they agree to disagree. But the damage had been done, as they both recalled every past perceived slight the other person uttered. The words left unsaid hung heavily between them, spoiling the friendship that had blossomed over shared interests, views, and (don't forget) gourmet popcorn. The argument may have been trivial on the surface to the outsider, but it was a chasm that neither of them chose to cross because of a pride clutched so tight it was bursting at the seams. As they continued their friendship in a strained manner, they both held onto the shadows of this argument. It was a small disagreement that left a significant dent, forever altering the fabric of their friendship.

HENRIETTA, MIKE, AND THE PROJECT TEAM

Mike and Henrietta were far more than just co-workers—they were a dynamic duo, a pair of seasoned professionals who worked together seamlessly. Their comradeship had been forged through the crucible of countless projects, each more challenging than the last. The shared late nights, the early mornings, and even the moments of frustration that came with the territory of their demanding work, had formed an unspoken bond between them. They had experienced the organization's team-building retreats, coming out stronger after every trust fall and group discussion (even that one time Mike failed to catch Henrietta . . . ouch).

Their dynamic was an exemplary one—a dance of ideas and solutions that moved in sync, with each partner respecting and appreciating the other's perspective. Therefore, Henrietta's surprise was profound when she found out that Mike had disagreed with her latest strategic proposal, a project that was close to her heart, to expand their organization's societal impact.

The news had come to her through the office grapevine, whispers of discontent murmuring through the corridors of their shared workspace. Her first reaction was disbelief, quickly followed by indignation and betrayal. Why had Mike not told her this himself? Why had he chosen to go behind her back, sharing his concerns with others instead of voicing them to her directly? She began to ponder how many other people might have felt this way and whether Mike was behind this misaligned mutiny.

The betrayal stung even more when she recalled how they had sat down together, poring over the proposal, discussing it in minute detail. At that time, Mike seemed to be fully on board, expressing his agreement with the directions she suggested. Had that been a facade?

As the shock subsided, Henrietta found herself speculating about the reasons behind Mike's actions. A rumor had been circulating about a looming promotion, and she was considered one of the leading candidates. Was it possible that Mike was envious? Could his actions have been a misguided attempt at sabotage?

Confused and hurt, Henrietta decided to maintain a professional relationship with Mike but kept their interactions to a minimum. She felt deeply betrayed and embarrassed by trusting Mike, and she heard her mother's voice in her head: "Never trust a man!" Not wanting to be labeled "emotional" and fearful of the fallout, Henrietta buried her feelings and never addressed the conflict. She avoided him whenever possible, a sharp contrast to the camaraderie they once shared.

Meanwhile, Mike was mystified. He noticed Henrietta's distance but couldn't understand the reason for it. It was only when the same colleague he had shared his concerns with revealed Henrietta's feelings that he understood the cause of the rift. Henrietta felt backstabbed, a consequence of his own actions that he hadn't anticipated.

Mike was a peacekeeper at heart, always opting for harmony over conflict. When he had disagreed with Henrietta's strategy, he chose not to confront her, fearing it might cause friction. His intention was to maintain the project's unity, keeping the team focused and motivated. He thought to himself that he should have just kept his mouth shut and not shared how he truly felt.

As the truth came out, Mike realized his silence had caused a misunderstanding. His fear of confrontation had inadvertently resulted in the very conflict he sought to avoid. Instead of simply respectfully disagreeing, he chose (for a myriad of reasons) to disrespectfully agree. It was a harsh lesson learned: the importance of clear communication and the consequences of avoiding difficult conversations. Yet, as he grappled with the fallout, he found himself unsure of how to rectify the situation. Could their partnership survive this unforeseen challenge, or had the dynamic duo danced their last dance together?

FAMILY AND FRACTURED FESTIVITIES

It was Christmas Eve, and the smell of cinnamon and roasted turkey wafted throughout the Baker household. Three generations of the Baker family were to gather for the holidays, a rare occasion since they were scattered across various states.

Jill Baker, the family matriarch, was excited. She had insisted on decorating every corner of the large home and cooked everyone's favorite dish with true delight. She always believed in the magic of Christmas, and for her, it was a time of joy and unity. However, she was not oblivious to the political divide that had formed among her children.

Her oldest, Sarah, was a journalist in New York and identified as a liberal. Sarah was passionate about her beliefs, often participating in protests and marches. Michael, the middle child, had taken over the family business and, with it, had developed conservative views. He often voiced his opinions on social media, much to the chagrin of Sarah. Lastly, there was Emily, the youngest, a college student and a self-proclaimed moderate—the Switzerland in family disputes.

When Sarah arrived, the atmosphere was still pleasant. Emily, always the peacemaker, had created a list of safe topics: movies, music, fashion, and technology. But as night fell and the wine flowed, the tension began to mount.

It began innocently enough. Michael commented on the economy and how the current administration had affected his business. Sarah, feeling the need to defend her stance, pointed out the social policies and how they impacted the less privileged. The conversation quickly spiraled. Emily tried to change the subject by asking about Sarah's new partner and Michael's recent vacation, but the damage was done.

Jill, seeing her children argue, felt a pang of sadness. It wasn't just about differing opinions; they were now questioning each other's intelligence and integrity. Michael accused Sarah of living in a media bubble, while Sarah retorted that he was nothing but a privileged elitist.

At the height of the argument, Jamie, Michael's eight-year-old son, broke down in tears. "Why are Aunt Sarah and Daddy yelling? Don't they love each other anymore?" he sobbed.

The room went silent. Emily took Jamie in her arms, comforting him while the others looked down in guilt. Jill, gathering her strength, finally spoke, "Look at what we've become.

We're a family. We might not always agree, but that doesn't give us the right to belittle each other. We must respect each other in the midst of our differences."

Sarah and Michael, reflecting on their behavior, felt ashamed. The weight of the moment was not lost on them. Both of them approached Jamie, apologized, and hugged him tightly.

The rest of the evening was subdued. The family played board games, sang carols, and shared fond memories. The political disagreements were still there, lurking beneath the surface, but they had realized something much more important—their love and respect for each other.

The night ended with a promise. While they might always have differing views, they would never let them get in the way of their bond. It was a lesson learned the hard way, but one they would never forget.

WHAT ABOUT YOU?

Can you spot your reflection in these three narratives? Perhaps you've never quarreled over a film choice with buttery popcorn (though I find that hard to believe), adopted a conciliatory role in a tense project meeting, or made a child weep over a holiday dinner. But chances are, you've experienced moments of quiet conflict. You've held your tongue at work, suppressing the urge to challenge an ill-considered remark for fear of disrupting the status quo. Or you've silently stewed at the Thanksgiving table, biting back a reply to a thoughtless statement aimed at an absent group.

Perhaps you find yourself at the opposite end of the spectrum—always dissenting or debating, your ceaseless challenges leading to repeated misunderstandings and tattered relationships both in real life and the digital realm. You might have found yourself struggling through childhood trauma and harmful structures of power, constantly feeling less than.

What if there were a different way forward? What we require is an infusion of humanity, a greater number of individuals willing to engage with others in ways that are constructive, empathetic, and ultimately humanizing.

These stories, these scenarios, hold a mirror to a profound truth about our interactions—one that is as vital to acknowledge as it is impossible to ignore. Disagreement is woven into the fabric of our existence, as inherent to our being as the air we inhale and the water we consume. Yet we frequently find ourselves ensnared in a cage of silence, stifling our thoughts, muffling our beliefs, paralyzed by the fear of disrupting harmony or inciting hostility.

Contrastingly, some of us are caught in an unending tempest of conflict, our dissenting views splintering relationships, causing misunderstandings, or even catalyzing estrangements. This predicament underlines the delicate balance we all attempt to strike—a precarious tightrope walk between the honest expression of our truths and the preservation of our valued relationships. While the conflicts we face are both big and small, what is constant is their frequency in our lives and their ability to leave a profound impact on us. Learning how to better handle these conflicts can help us have better conversations, relationships, and workplaces. This is our WHY!

How Do You See People?

How do you perceive people? Equally important, how do you perceive yourself? Your perception of yourself and others fundamentally influences how you interact with people, especially in moments of disagreement. Can you look at another person, regardless of knowing their wealth, status, or power, and see them (and treat them) as your equal? Can you recognize the inherent value in everyone, and treat them with the dignity, honor, and respect they deserve?

Though we might never mold a utopia of perfect respect (apologies to fans of the Berenstain Bears), we can strive for progress. We can become the change we want to see in the world in small yet meaningful ways. We will always have "difficult" people in our lives, but as the authors of *The Anatomy of Peace* (and ferocious researchers of human connectedness) poignantly note, "Difficult people are nevertheless people."[1] Now, the question is, are you ready to diver deeper? Are you ready to grow your perspective and cultivate a deep-seated respect that transcends disagreements? If your answer is yes, I invite you to open your heart and mind and continue reading, and let's set sail on this transformative voyage together. If your answer is no, well, I didn't like you anyway . . . haha! On a serious note, no matter where you are currently, I invite you to grow forward with me. One part of growing forward is to know how we respond to conflict.

The Four Responses of Conversation Conflict

When we are in conflict, we are often unaware of how layered and complex our behaviors are. As human beings we project our inner issues all over the place, and knowing this can empower us to build patience, empathy, self-awareness, and accountability when we disagree.

As it relates to the agreement/disagreement and respectful/disrespectful continuums, my colleagues and I have found four responses to conversation conflict (refer back to figure 1 in the part I opener):

RESPECTFULLY DISAGREEING My goal is to help you spend more time in this quadrant.

RESPECTFULLY AGREEING This is not the primary focus of this book, but it's a potential outcome of respectful communication.

DISRESPECTFULLY DISAGREEING I aim to help you spend less time here.

DISRESPECTFULLY AGREEING This is a surprising trouble spot, where you disrespect either yourself or the person you're supposedly agreeing with.

Our goal is to spend more time respectfully disagreeing, as research shows doing so "can help us increase the accuracy of our own beliefs by exposing us to new information and perspectives."[2] It also strengthens our friendships, invigorates our workplaces, and reduces familial tension.

So why is respectful disagreement so hard? One challenge is our need to do things perfectly, but perfection is not the goal. Remember this. We will never be perfect; instead, our aim is progress. People will do all they can to stay in a false state of harmony. One study revealed that participants chose to forgo receiving money to avoid effort, frustration, and potential relationship damage—all commendable in the pursuit of harmony. It also found that people were slightly more interested in taking out the trash than hearing from their ideological other. The good news is that people were slightly more open to hearing from the other side than standing in line for twenty minutes and definitely would rather hear from the other side than get their teeth pulled.[3] There is hope for us, after all! The practical hope I espouse in this book is the 5 Pillars Model of Bridging the Divide:

Pillar 1: Challenge Your Perspective

Pillar 2: Be the Student

Pillar 3: Cultivate Your Curiosity

Pillar 4: Seek the Gray

Pillar 5: Agree to Respect

These pillars matter because they move us forward in a practical way from saying things like, "Can't we all just get along?" to disagreeing with others more respectfully. In part II I'll go through each pillar in detail and how to practically apply it in everyday life. It is vitally important for us to bridge the divide, because when we don't, we are building up barriers, which significantly hurts our relationships, workplaces, and even our mental health at times. When we build up barriers, we close ourselves off from valuing the humanity of others. My hope is that you will spend less and less time building up barriers when you disagree with others. I will discuss this further in chapter 4.

Moving from Disrespectful to Respectful

From these pillars, my team has designed practical strategies to transition from disrespectfully (dis)agreeing to respectfully disagreeing. Passive aggressiveness has pervaded organizational and working life and has hurt our ability to have meaningful and respectful disagreements. Not only do we sometimes demean others in our disagreements, but we also disrespect others and ourselves when we pretend to agree! In this book and through the pillars, I provide hope and a way to counter that. Table 1-1 includes a few examples of transitioning to respectful disagreement.

In a world that often seems more divided than united, this book is your companion for creating connections, not chasms, through respectful disagreement.

TABLE 1-1: How to Respectfully Disagree

DISRESPECTFULLY (DIS)AGREEING	RESPECTFULLY DISAGREEING
Cutting people off and jumping into the conversation	Allowing a person to share their full view and perspective (Pillars 1 and 2)
Only considering examples that bolster your view	Looking for all relevant facts and information and empathetically considering their view (Pillar 2)
Only focusing on what you want to share and give to them	Focusing on both learning and sharing (Pillars 2 and 5)
Assuming what people "really" mean or are thinking	Asking questions for greater clarity and understanding (Pillar 3)
Seeing only where you disagree and all the negative aspects of the disagreement	Finding the shared perspective and where there might be alignment (Pillar 4)
Externally sharing that you agree when internally you disagree	Sharing your truth with a posture to always acknowledge the other (Pillar 5)

REFLECTIONS AND ACTIONS

1. Reflect on a time you felt disrespectfully disagreed with. What did it feel like, and what did you wish the person did differently?

2. Which of the six ways to respectfully disagree (table 1-1) stands out to you the most and why?

3. At first glance, which of the pillars is the most appealing to you and why?

CHAPTER 2

Why I Respectfully Disagree
with Aretha Franklin

The Choice of Golden Respect

This chapter redefines respect from how society characterizes it into a more humanizing version. You will learn how to make the powerful choice to lean into Golden Respect and identify ways that you can spend more time in Golden Respect with others. We'll begin with a story.

Tasha had always looked up to her mother, Pamela, as a pillar of strength and wisdom. Pamela, being the eldest among her siblings, naturally took charge in many family situations. Her leadership tendencies were amplified as her parents often leaned on her during challenging times, giving her responsibilities that were beyond her years. This responsibility had molded Pamela, ingraining in her a natural instinct to guide, protect, and, often, instruct.

When Tasha became a mother herself, she had hoped to lean on her mother for support. But soon, that support took on a form that Tasha hadn't expected. Every phone call, every

Sunday dinner, every casual meetup became an opportunity for Pamela to provide unsolicited advice. It seemed Pamela always had something to say about how Tasha was raising her children, be it their diet, bedtime routines, or Tasha's discipline methods.

While Tasha respected her mother's wisdom and even agreed with some of her advice, it was the relentless nature of these remarks that wore thin. It began to feel as if her every move as a parent was under scrutiny.

Attempts to shield herself from her mother's constant criticism led Tasha to develop a defense mechanism: responding sarcastically. An "Of course, Mother" here, a "Thanks for the insight" there—these remarks, meant to deflect, only deepened the rift between them.

Tasha felt overshadowed and undermined, while Pamela, in her mind, was merely trying to help. This tug-of-war strained their relationship to the point where Tasha began avoiding her mother. Her children, sensing the underlying tension, grew wary around their grandmother.

One afternoon, after a disagreement about the children's study habits, Tasha finally vented her frustration. "Mom, can't you trust me to make the right decisions for my kids? Why must every conversation turn into a critique?"

Pamela, taken aback, responded, "I just want what's best for you and the grandchildren. I've faced challenges, and I want to save you from the same pitfalls." Pamela also believed that being Tasha's mother granted her the right to respect, which to her meant Tasha not only listening but also implementing her advice.

Tasha's voice trembled with emotion. "But I need to learn, just like you did. I can't grow if you're always guiding my every step."

Their bond, once unshakable, now seemed on the brink of fracturing. Tasha's husband, David, suggested family counseling. "You both need a neutral space to communicate without judgment," he proposed.

Pamela, though initially hesitant about discussing personal matters with an outsider, eventually recognized the gravity of their deteriorating relationship and agreed.

The counseling sessions were challenging. They confronted past issues, shared their fears, and voiced their grievances. With the counselor's guidance, they began to understand each other's perspective. Pamela tried to curtail her instinct to intervene, while Tasha learned to communicate her feelings more openly.

Their bond took time to mend, and while disagreements were inevitable, they approached them with newfound respect and understanding. They realized that while experience is valuable, every generation has its path to carve, and sometimes, it's okay for the young tree to grow in its own direction. After one counseling session, on the way home, they jammed to Aretha Franklin's song "Respect," and Tasha looked at her mom with a playful smile and mouthed the lyric "just a little bit!" They both burst into laughter and continued to dance.

R-E-S-P-E-C-T

Were you taken aback by this chapter's title? Hold on, now, before your mind races ahead to assumptions and casts the first "rolling stone," let me clarify something! I hold the late Aretha Franklin, the incontestable Queen of Soul, in the highest regard. If her name is unfamiliar to you, I implore you to embark on the exciting journey of learning about her music and legacy.

One point where we might differ, however, concerns her iconic song "Respect" (for those not acquainted with this classic, please take a moment to bask in its powerful rhythm and poignant lyrics). As someone who frequently attends conferences and delivers keynote speeches, I've noticed how this song often emerges in conversations about respect. Now, before the music aficionados raise their eyebrows at me, I am fully aware that the song's context vastly diverges from my interpretation. Yet diving into the lyrics proves a fascinating exercise.

I love this song but have one small disagreement with it. The song sees Aretha passionately demanding "a little respect" when her man comes home. It's all in that word *little*. I posit that today's society doesn't need a little respect; it demands *a lot* of respect! But with the varying interpretations of respect in today's world, it also seems necessary to articulate its meaning.

NOTE Here's a bit of trivia for you: Did you know that Aretha Franklin wasn't the original composer of "Respect"? The credit goes to Otis Redding, who wrote and performed it back in 1965. But when Aretha got her hands on it two years later, she imprinted it with her distinct style, creating a version that eclipsed the original. It was a rendition so profound that *Rolling Stone* declared it the greatest song of all time. Now that's a description that stirs up some disagreement!

GOLDEN RESPECT: THE CHOICE IS YOURS

Not only do we need a lot of respect, we need a lot of the *right type* of respect. Society has given respect many definitions, but I would like to offer my own. Respect, to me, is acknowledging and valuing the shared humanity of each individual.

Allow me to elucidate by presenting the 10 Characteristics of Golden Respect in table 2-1, which compares society's standard interpretation of respect and the tenets of what I call Golden Respect.

TABLE 2-1: The 10 Characteristics of Golden Respect

SOCIETAL VIEWS ON RESPECT	GOLDEN RESPECT
1 You must earn respect.	Everyone should be given respect, value, and dignity.
2 You only give respect when it is given to you; otherwise, you are weak and a pushover.	We make the courageous and strong choice to give respect, whether or not it is reciprocated.
3 Respect means agreeing with others when you don't.	Respect means being honest with ourselves and others, filtered through a heart to help and not harm.
4 Respect means being in awe of a person and holding them in high regard.	You value the humanity of the person even if you do not like them, what they represent, or what they believe.
5 Respect means being passive. You can't be critical and express a different opinion or perspective, especially to those in power.	Golden Respect allows for being assertive. Providing alternative perspectives is good, while also valuing others and hearing their perspective.
6 Respect is about being "nice," "polite," and diplomatic to all people (external focus) without regard for what you really feel and think (how-to only).	Rather than creating a misalignment between your external behaviors and internal feelings, the goal of Golden Respect is sharing your truth in love, with a heart to help and not harm the other person (how-to and why-to).

TABLE 2-1: The 10 Characteristics of Golden Respect (*Continued*)

	SOCIETAL VIEWS ON RESPECT	GOLDEN RESPECT
7	Being respectful means avoiding conflict at all costs.	Golden Respect sees healthy conflict as a means for growth.
8	A person's title grants them respect.	A person's humanity grants them respect.
9	Respect means being obedient to those in authority.	Golden Respect means fully acknowledging that the person you disagree with has the power to choose their perspective.
10	Respect is about eye contact and open body language.	While nonverbal cues can indicate how a person feels, Golden Respect is more about the heart than external cues.

We often struggle to "respect" others because we've been trained by society's definitions, but what if we embraced a new one? Golden Respect is the ideal; it's not simply taking the old misperceptions of respect and adding to them, but rather redefining respect to enable a new way of communicating. Yes, you might have adopted a few or many of the tenets of Golden Respect, but my goal is that you consistently make the choice to respect others in this way. This is respect in a whole new light!

The old adage "respect is earned" paints an image of respect as some sort of currency, something to strive for and obtain. This presents respect as a quid pro quo arrangement, where you only give it if you get it. I respectfully disagree with this characterization; in my humble opinion, respect is a gift we choose to offer others. Golden Respect is a combination of courage and conviction. When we respect others, we are doing something not only for them but also for ourselves by acknowledging our shared humanity.

Power and Respect

Although this book is not the antidote to power differentials in our relationships, I want to draw your attention briefly to this pervasive dynamic as it relates to respect. Disagreements are an intrinsic part of human interactions, driven by our varied perceptions, beliefs, needs, and desires. But beneath the overt layers of disagreement often lies the silent yet potent force of power differentials. Power, in its myriad forms, can both covertly and overtly shape the nature and outcome of our disagreements.

Power is the ability to influence the behavior of others to achieve desired outcomes. Its forms are varied. Coercive power, for instance, is derived from the ability to punish. In contrast, reward power emerges from positive reinforcement. Expert power is rooted in one's specific expertise or knowledge that others may not possess. Referent power arises when an individual is admired or respected, and others want to identify with them. Lastly, legitimate power is derived from a recognized position of authority, such as a manager in a company.[1]

When disagreements occur, the dynamics of power play a significant role. If one party possesses more power, whether it's real or perceived, they often control the narrative. This control could mean they get to set the terms of the discussion, downplay or outright dismiss the concerns of the less powerful, or heavily influence the outcome in a way that aligns with their desires.

Awareness of power differentials is essential for several reasons. For one, only when there's an even playing field can disagreements be resolved in a manner that's genuinely fair to both parties. The party with more power may lead the resolution process in a direction that heavily favors them, even if it's not the most just or equitable outcome. Moreover, when there's an imbalance in power, it can deter open dialogue. The party with less power might hesitate to voice their concerns or needs out of fear or perceived futility, leading to unresolved issues or suppressed feelings. Additionally, power imbalances, when persistent, can severely impact the emotional well-being of the less powerful party. Feelings of stress, anxiety, or helplessness can arise. Lastly, for the sake of maintaining healthy interpersonal relationships, recognizing and addressing power imbalances is vital. If left unchecked, long-standing power imbalances can erode trust and mutual respect, turning the relationship toxic.

Recognition is the first step. Individuals must be self-aware, especially if they are in a position of power during a disagreement. This awareness shouldn't be a tool to further self-interests but to ensure the discourse remains fair. An integral aspect of addressing these imbalances is through empathetic listening. It's essential to genuinely attempt to understand the feelings and concerns of the less powerful party. In situations where the power differential is pronounced, seeking mediation from a neutral third party can be beneficial. This neutral party can provide perspective, ensuring fairness in resolution. Another effective approach is shared decision-making. Making decisions collaboratively can minimize the effects of power imbalances, ensuring all parties feel involved and valued.

The final point is the perspective with which we view power: in the context of disagreements, power shouldn't be approached as a tool to achieve victory but instead as a responsibility. Those endowed with more power—whether due to position, knowledge, or some other factor—have a responsibility to ensure fairness, understanding, and respect in the discourse. Power dynamics subtly yet significantly influence disagreements. Recognizing these dynamics and working to ensure power doesn't overshadow the core of a disagreement can help us spend more time respectfully disagreeing.

Sometimes we avoid leaning into respectful disagreement because of exhaustion or fear of retaliation, being blacklisted, or worse. In order to create workplaces and communities where people can respectfully dissent, leaders should aspire to model this behavior. This applies not only to power and respect but also to culture and respect.

Culture and Respect

Let's talk about how cultures shape our perception of respect. For instance, where I grew up, playful trash talk was seen as a sign of mutual respect and camaraderie. My family loved to tease and poke fun at each other, forming a unique bond through this shared humor. But when I tried the same approach with people from different backgrounds, it often led to misunderstandings and hurt feelings. I quickly realized that cultural experiences shape perceptions of respect, and mine wasn't the universal standard. This was a significant moment of growth and learning for me.

Another example of the intersection of culture and respect comes from Japan. I have learned much from my mother, who spent some significant time there before I was born, and from a Japanese exchange student. She taught me that respect was conveyed in the depth of your bow, how you address your elders, how you give and receive gifts, and how seniority is addressed at work. One way of showing respect in Japan that would have been challenging in my childhood home is silence. In traditional Japanese culture, silence is a form of respect, and remaining silent and thinking before you speak are seen as critical (I could use a little more of that!). In my household growing up, there was no such thing as silence—everyone had an opinion and shared it freely and loud! I am quite sure our Japanese exchange student thought we were very rude and disrespectful to each other, and this is why it's vital to understand the cultural nuances of respect.

A pressing issue in businesses and communities today is the culture of "surface-level respect," or passive aggressiveness. We nod and agree in meetings, avoiding conflict at all costs, yet we harbor resentment, judgments, and real disagreements in our hearts. This facade of polite agreement is nothing more than a mask hiding our true feelings. It raises the question: Are we merely humoring people or are we truly humanizing them?

Respect goes beyond words; it encompasses how you say things and, more importantly, why you say them. It's about your intent. Have you ever had a leader say that everyone's voice is valued but then question only certain groups of people? The term *respect* has been given lip service instead of real consideration.

The notion of respect also extends beyond agreement. It's not about mirroring someone's views but about acknowledging their perspective. As a parent, I've had my fair share of disagreements with my kids, but that doesn't undermine the respect we have for each other. Heck, I disagreed quite a bit with my mom, but I still respected her (most of the time . . . sorry, Mom). Respect also isn't about maintaining the status quo and avoiding conflict at the cost of injustices.

Respectful Disagreement Is Not Politeness

Sometimes people use the concept of respect subconsciously or consciously to stifle the progress of others. During the civil rights era in the mid-twentieth century, some parts of the United States would condemn so-called outsiders for not being polite and for challenging the known way of life, even though it was harmful to people of color.

Now, this may raise a question: Should we protest what we feel is unfair? My answer would be a resounding yes. However, we should protest ideologies, not individuals. Assigning labels to people tends to dehumanize them, while questioning their views paves the way for understanding and growth. This lesson can also be seen in couples counseling, which encourages focusing on the actions of your partner rather than verbally attacking them.[2] Research on the subject found that verbal attacks were ineffective for behavior change and actually created more barriers between the two parties.

Navigating the complex dynamics of respect can be tricky. It's common for people to equate disagreement with disrespect, especially in hierarchical settings. Let me share an example that's fictional but plays out all too often in our everyday world.

Jonathan, the Disrespectful Leader

In the heart of Middle America stood the towering offices of Global Finance Corp, a multinational investment firm known for its aggressive market strategies. At the helm was Jonathan Walker, a stern individual known for his unwavering convictions and a staunch belief in his own viewpoints.

Jonathan was a highly intelligent and capable leader. He was known for his quick decision-making and insightful understanding of the market. However, he had one glaring flaw: he viewed disagreement as a form of disrespect. To Jonathan, questioning his decisions was akin to challenging his authority—a view he had learned the hard way in his home growing up.

This trait was especially evident during the weekly team meetings. In these sessions, Jonathan would outline his strategies and plans for the upcoming weeks. Even though he invited everyone to voice their opinions, what he really wanted was quite different.

One day, Sophia, a junior analyst, mustered the courage to question one of Jonathan's decisions about an upcoming investment. She presented a well-researched argument, stating that the investment had potential risks that had been overlooked.

Jonathan's face immediately hardened. The room went silent. To him, Sophia's well-intentioned disagreement felt like a direct challenge to his authority. He fired back with a condescending remark, publicly shaming Sophia for having the audacity to question his judgment.

The message was clear and powerful. From that day forward, team members feared voicing any contrary opinions, even when they spotted a flaw in Jonathan's plans. Their self-censorship did not stem from respect for Jonathan's expertise but from fear of his retaliation. Creativity, critical thinking, and healthy debate, all of which had previously thrived, began to disappear.

The impact on Global Finance Corp was disastrous. The company started to make blunders, missing out on profitable opportunities and making risky moves due to the lack of thorough deliberation. Morale dipped as employees felt their professional input was undervalued. The attrition rate rose alarmingly, with many employees feeling stifled in the oppressive atmosphere.

Jonathan's belief that disagreement was a sign of disrespect led to a monologue culture within the company, where alternative perspectives were not just unheard, but actively silenced. By failing to distinguish between dissent and disrespect, he pushed Global Finance Corp into a downward spiral of missed opportunities and diminished employee satisfaction.

It's easy to forget that respect isn't deserved simply because of the position we occupy. When we're secure in who we are as leaders, we are able to encourage respectful dissent (which is not the same as always agreeing) from our colleagues and reports. We have a responsibility to encourage a culture of respectful disagreement instead of seeking constant validation. When we do this, we create better work environments where people want to be and can help our organizations thrive.

NOTE For more leadership tips, see Resource 2 later in the book.

But let's not forget that respect doesn't mean we offer equal airtime to all opinions, especially when it comes to issues with clear evidence supporting one side over the other, such as the harmful impact of child trafficking or abuse. For example, if someone is defending an abuser, it may be important to understand what happened in their life to bring them to this viewpoint, but this does not require giving them the same airtime as a person sharing how abuse is harmful to the victim and to society at large.

While these examples are large societal issues, in our personal interactions, we should be willing to listen and understand differing viewpoints. This isn't about promoting false balance, but about nurturing understanding and empathy. While institutional systems and structures are vastly important to the topic of respect and disagreements, they are not the focus of this book. We are focused on the interpersonal relationships at home, work, and in the community that continue to be fractured because of disrespectful disagreements and disrespectful agreements.

Personality and Respect

Lastly, let's talk about personality and respect. Often, people with straightforward and task-oriented personalities are perceived as disrespectful due to their direct approach. It's important to remember that we all have unique social styles, and it's crucial not to confuse personality traits with disrespect. My friend Dave is constantly explaining himself because he is so direct and straight to the point. On more than one occasion, the organization where he is a leader has sat him down to address what they see as disrespect. To be clear, Dave has some work to do in better engaging the "people side" of the organization, but the organization has some work to do as well in not conflating Dave and his "driver" personality with disrespect.[3]

Our personalities have also been informed by past and current traumas, which deeply affect how we relate to others and how we act when we encounter a perceived threat or perceived disrespect (such as shutting down or fighting).

Respecting someone who disrespects you might be one of the toughest things to do, but it's absolutely possible. And that's the beauty of respect—it's a choice, a gift we can offer others, regardless of their actions. It might not be easy, but like the tortoise we can choose to move forward steadily, giving this gift to others.

Remember, it's about recognizing our shared humanity and acting accordingly.

How to Respect Others When They Disrespect Us

We often encounter threads of disrespect that threaten to fray the fabric of our shared humanity. This situation can be challenging, but it also presents an opportunity to extend respect even when it's not reciprocated.

Viktor Frankl, a man whose life was steeped in some of the harshest realities of the human experience, knew this well. A Holocaust survivor, Frankl penned the wisdom gleaned from his experiences in his powerful book *Man's Search for Meaning*.[4] He wrote of the depths of human cruelty, but also of the heights of human resilience and dignity. His journey through unimaginable adversity led him to a startling realization: even when stripped of all other freedoms, we still retain the freedom to choose our attitude, to choose our response.

Even in the dehumanizing reality of a Nazi concentration camp, Frankl chose to respect the humanity in everyone—not because he condoned their actions, but because he recognized the value of every human life. To him, respect wasn't about acceptance or agreement, but about acknowledging the inherent worth of each individual and our choice to see their humanity.

In the book Frankl states, "Everything can be taken from a man but one thing: the last of the human freedoms—to choose one's attitude in any given set of circumstances, to choose one's own way." Therein lies the compelling wisdom we can embrace in our own lives. When faced with disrespect, we can choose to meet it with respect—not as an endorsement of another's behavior, but as a reflection of our own values. We can choose to see the humanity in others, even when they fail to see ours. Again, I'm not suggesting this is an easy task, but it remains our choice. I sincerely hope that you'll never be in a position or face an experience like Frankl's, but we can take inspiration from his story.

American civil rights figure Rosa Parks, former president of South Africa Nelson Mandela (who we will discuss in chapter 4), and Pakistani education activist Malala Yousafzai are other examples of people who moved forward with their causes while still choosing to respect (not agree with) others in the process.

Respect Is a Choice

Another example is the story of Patrick Hutchinson. During a 2020 Black Lives Matter protest in London, Hutchinson, a Black man, came to the aid of a white counterprotester, Bryn Male, who had been injured. Despite their political differences, Hutchinson saw a fellow human being in distress and took action. He lifted Male onto his shoulders, shielding him from the angry crowd, and carried him to safety.[5]

His selfless act, captured in a photograph that spread worldwide, stands as a testament to the power of respect and compassion. Hutchinson chose not to mirror the hostility he was faced with. Instead, he responded with humanity. His respect for another human life didn't hinge on the reciprocation of that respect.

Respecting others when they disrespect us is, without doubt, a challenging choice. It requires us to reject the urge for retaliation or submission, and instead embrace the strength within ourselves to respond with dignity and compassion. Yet, in doing so, we not only enrich our own character but also affirm the shared humanity that connects us all.

We can't control how others perceive or treat us. Let me ask you a question: Who is the only person that you and I can control? Our kids or pets? (Nope, I've tried and it doesn't work!) But we can control ourselves. In every interaction, we have the power to choose respect over disrespect, love over hate, understanding over judgment. In this choice, we find the freedom to shape our own narrative and the opportunity to inspire change, one respectful act at a time.

Respect doesn't need to be earned; it is given, as a testament to our own choice of humanity. This is the essence of respect when faced with disrespect: It's not about them. It's about us. As Viktor Frankl says, "The more one forgets himself—by giving himself to a cause to serve or another person to love—the more human he is."[6]

DISAGREEMENT DEFINED

Consider this statement: "A dog is a man's best friend." Do you agree? For sure, the people in ninety-one countries who prefer cats over dogs and the 25.4 percent of American households that own cats might vehemently object, possibly even hurling this book across the room![7] But stick with me. The point isn't about canine supremacy; it's about exploring how we handle disagreements.

The Cambridge English Dictionary defines *disagreement* as "an argument or a situation in which people do not have the same opinion."[8] These differences of opinion are often a source of discord and discomfort. Disagreements, silly or serious, can seriously strain our relationships.

The degree of disagreement can range from mild to severe and can be affected by how much we care about the subject at hand. We sometimes brush off a discussion not because we're apathetic, but because we fear the potential unease it might cause. Sometimes we simply want to avoid disagreements at all costs. People would rather "ghost" someone (cutting off all communication with someone suddenly and without explanation) than express disagreement.

As a society, we might find disagreement unpalatable, yet we're strangely fascinated by others' disputes. I recall from my time as a radio host how my most heated and contentious shows attracted the highest ratings. Yet I found that these exchanges were rarely respectful and, to be transparent, they were rarely constructive.

In the face of disagreement, a common refrain is "let's agree to disagree." While seemingly diplomatic, this statement can be misinterpreted as dismissing the other's viewpoint, and you can still agree to disagree disrespectfully, which isn't very constructive. Sometimes this phrase is simply an easy escape route to sidestep uncomfortable conversations.

SEED PLANTERS, NOT PEOPLE CHANGERS

We need to see ourselves as seed planters, not opinion changers. Recall a time when someone considered your opposing view thoughtfully. How did it make you feel? Our goal should be to cultivate understanding, rather than seeking victory in our disagreements. So the next time you're in a disagreement, think of it as an opportunity to plant a seed of understanding rather than as a battle to be won.

Respectful disagreement isn't about converting others to our way of thinking. It's about acknowledging their dignity, value, and worth, even when their ideas clash with ours. Modeling this respect encourages receptiveness in dialogue, according to research.[9] Like a heartfelt apology in a heated argument, this approach can break down barriers, promoting understanding and empathy. To be clear, not all disagreements are the same, but we always have a choice in how we engage.

Disagreeing is a natural part of our human interactions. The way we navigate these situations reflects our values, beliefs, and attitudes. This is often based on what was modeled for us and what happened to us growing up. Join me in chapter 3 to dive deeper into this topic.

REFLECTIONS AND ACTIONS

1. Which of the 10 Characteristics of Golden Respect resonate the most to you and why?

2. What is one thing you can do in your next disagreement to show the other person respect?

3. Think of a time when either you or someone you know enhanced their perspective because of respect given during a disagreement. What happened?

CHAPTER 3

A Picture of the Past

A Catalyst for Who You Are Today

This chapter takes a deep dive into how past experiences, childhood hurts, and even familial patterns influence how you approach disagreements. Understanding your past will help you move into a future of more respectful disagreements. In this chapter, allow yourself to go back in time to determine what's blocking you from the choice of Golden Respect and to start making progress toward more respect in your disagreements.

It should come as no surprise that the threads that stitch together the tapestry of your life are deeply connected to your origins, to every moment you've lived and experienced from the day of your birth until this very second. This is true of my story, too. I was born in Detroit, but following my parents' divorce when I was just four years old, my mother, older brother, and I moved to Grand Rapids, Michigan. Our new life was marked by moments of financial instability, a brief stint of homelessness, and the personal shame of being on welfare.

Among the multitude of moments that helped chisel me into the person I am today, the most influential were, unfortunately, not the most pleasant ones. Rather, they were the ones filled with anguish and torment, with the physical and emotional abuse I suffered at the hands of my brother, who was eight years older than me and had a different father. This wasn't the harmless squabbling you'd typically associate with sibling rivalry.

I remember vividly how my brother would blame me for almost everything that didn't go as planned. His wrath felt merciless, scarring me more than any words could describe. I recall one incident when he got in trouble for something concerning me. He whispered, his breath hot against my ear, threatening me with his impending retaliation once our mother left the house. Even recalling it today causes a shudder down my spine, a lump in my throat, and tears in my eyes.

That evening, our mother had a book club meeting. As a single mother, she scarcely had time for herself, and these rare moments of solitude were her treasured escape. Terrified of what my brother would do to me, I begged her to take me along, promised her that I'd be good, that I wouldn't cause any disturbance. But my pleas were not heard. Fearful of worsening my situation, I didn't dare to reveal the true reason behind my desperate pleas. My brother was my primary caregiver most of the time due to our circumstances.

Unable to accompany my mother, I decided to go to bed before she left, under the hopeful illusion that my brother wouldn't harm me in my sleep. I quickly dove into my twin-size bed in our rented home and managed to drift off. However, I was jolted awake on the floor, the taste of blood filling my mouth. My brother had struck me so brutally that I was thrown off the bed. When my mother returned and found me bloodied, I lied and told her I had fallen down the stairs. I felt so powerless, so isolated, so vulnerable.

Fast-forward fifteen years, when I finally confessed to my mother about the years of torment I had endured at my brother's hands. I was inspired to tell her what happened to me after I'd shared my story in a college speech class. Dr. Stephens and that class helped me uncover how my upbringing shaped who I'd become—both good and bad—and understand the lingering effects of the abuse I'd suffered. (To be completely transparent with you, I am crying as I type this, as I can still feel how I felt as that six-year-old boy.)

By this point, I had already forgiven my brother, a choice that I made because of what I uncovered during that unforgettable and very emotional speech class. I had to look deep within, and I did all I could to employ empathy strategies to better understand what led my brother to abuse me. Was it the absence of his dad, was it perceived neglect from his stepfather (my biological dad), or did he just see me as a nuisance? No matter how he got there, I had the power to choose to forgive him, even if I disagreed with his actions.

Forgiveness is the perfect ally to respectful disagreement, because it doesn't take anyone other than you to do it. Do you see the liberty here? My brother never asked for my forgiveness, but I *chose* to forgive him, because it was imprisoning me with toxic emotions and feelings. Forgiveness was about me, not him! To be able to forgive in that way took consistent work on myself, a great therapist, and a choice to move forward. It wasn't easy, but it was and is doable.

Today, when I look back at my past, the pieces of the puzzle fit together; the reasons behind my instinctual "fight" mode become clearer. For years, I couldn't comprehend why

I always felt the need to protect myself, to defend my territory. I had to win every argument, and if I had a big disagreement with someone, I made it personal and resorted to verbal attacks. I had to attack them first before they could come after me. Now, I realize that I was battling for that terrified little boy who'd had no way of defending himself. I was determined to never let anyone get the upper hand over me again, whether it was in a heated argument or a physical altercation. I now had the power to protect myself from all "attackers." This was a direct outcome of the traumatic experiences I had undergone.

Thank you for letting me share my story. Why did I share it? First, I want to lead with vulnerability and show you that I, too, am impacted by my experiences, traumas, and life story. Second, I want you to lean into your own story and how you have experienced life and disagreement. You likely don't have the same story I have, but you've had your own set of challenges and experiences. Without understanding your own story, you'll find it very challenging to respectfully disagree with others from the heart rather than just performing the act. As you think of your story, consider how you can learn from it, grow from it, and become better because of it. You are still alive and moving, and we all have the power of choice to keep learning!

One takeaway from this story is the power of forgiveness. I do not believe I would be able to respectfully disagree to this degree had I not processed forgiveness toward my brother (and my dad, who you will read about in the upcoming chapters). Getting to this place of Golden Respect requires some heart work, which will allow us to use the information we are given in a way that honors ourselves and respects others!

Before we continue, a word of caution: Some of what I ask you in this next section may be triggering. If so, take a pause from the book and come back to it when you are able. If it gets really challenging, please consider contacting a trained therapist who can help you walk through what you are feeling and thinking.

LIFE DISAGREEMENT MARKERS

Every human being is acting and reacting based on their own life experiences. When we develop this awareness, we can react a little less and respect a lot more. What are the significant moments from your childhood, school years, and early professional life that have influenced the way you approach disagreements today? What are the meaningful moments in your life, both positive and negative, that have played a role in shaping how you handle disagreements today? Life Disagreement Markers (LDMs) are the moments in our lives, both good and bad, that have influenced how we see and process disagreements. Being aware of them can be helpful in determining how we move forward in our disagreements.

Now, sit back and dive deep into your past, traversing the different stages of your life. Think of your infancy, toddlerhood, childhood, adolescence, adulthood, middle age, and older age. If you want to dive in deeper, reflect on each stage for three to five minutes and see what comes up. Try to recall the moments that have shaped you—those pivotal, unforgettable instances that have influenced the way you disagree. Not every stage may hold significant memories, and that's all right. Focus on the best of times, and on those challenging moments that might have affected how you handle disagreements.

Some of you might find that this brings up uncomfortable memories, much like it did for me. It's challenging to understand others (and to respectfully disagree) if we don't better understand ourselves; this is why identifying your LDMs can be such a powerful exercise.

For those of you who connect more with visual representation, consider creating a picture of what disagreement looks like for you today. Drawing can be an excellent alternative to taking a linear approach to your life journey, with benefits like improving memory recall, promoting mindfulness, and enhancing nonverbal communication. Engaging our past in a multitude of ways can help us map a path toward a better understanding of our present and future selves.

FAMILY PATTERNS

The family home: It's a master class, an incubator of the self, shaping and molding the individuals we become. It's where we first learn how to navigate disagreements, the subtle art of debate, the delicate dance of communication. Think back to your childhood. What did conflict look like in your home? Was it loud and ferocious, or veiled and passive? The patterns of our past echo in our present, influencing how we react to and manage conflicts in our own lives.

When you were a child, maybe you were told to hug an elder even when you didn't want to. Such instances taught you to bury your dissent, to bottle up your discomfort. You learned that disagreement led to conflict, and conflict was something to avoid at all costs. And now, as an adult, you might find yourself struggling with the same. It becomes a vicious cycle of conditioning, one that can be extremely hard to break.

During disagreements you might have seen your parents or guardians hurling insults in a shouting match (or even worse). Maybe you were that child who ran the household and was treated as a "bonus" adult. You had to take care of everyone else and make tough decisions, which may have led to you being uncomfortable when things don't go your way. We often underestimate how much our upbringing impacts how we function today.

But that's not all. Our upbringing also colors our perceptions of others—it defines our in-group and out-group. And this division, often subtle, can slowly transform into a subconscious sense of superiority, a bias that can influence our interactions. Some members of my extended family, for instance, ingrained in me a sense of prejudice against interracial couples (specifically Black women with white men), a bias that I actively combat today. If we are honest with ourselves, we all have patterns we live by, both good and bad, that were influenced by our family. However, acknowledging these biases and patterns is the first step toward breaking them. When we're aware of the patterns we have learned over time, we can actively choose to learn and grow from our interactions.

Think about the biases you might harbor. Do you see yourself as superior to certain groups—the poor, the rich, those without a degree, or even those who don't keep their lawn as perfect as you do? Remember, superiority isn't always blatant—it can be insidious, creeping into our subconscious and subtly influencing our interactions. It's not about power or prestige, it's about dehumanizing others. It takes away from our shared humanity, creating division where there should be unity.

Imagine if we could shift our mindset so that, rather than falling into the familiar patterns of fight or flight during disagreements, we sought insight instead. What if we recognized these conflicts as opportunities to understand another's perspective better, to deepen our empathy and broaden our perspectives?

This conscious choice to engage rather than retreat, to question rather than accept, to connect rather than alienate—that is the real power of respectful disagreement. It's not about winning or losing, but about understanding and growing. This is not easy and sometimes requires more work on ourselves. Sometimes all we can manage is to simply survive the day . . . I have been there. Instead of focusing on the big changes, then, let's frame our perspective for the small changes of how we grow. This, my dear reader, is an important part of Pillar 1: Challenge Your Perspective, the details of which we'll dive into in the upcoming chapters.

But remember, this process is not about striving for perfection, but about acknowledging our biases, challenging the familial patterns that hold us back, and taking those crucial steps towards empathy, understanding, and respectful disagreement. So, are you ready to embark on this journey with me? We'll start by questioning the patterns we've held onto for far too long. Let's dive in!

NAÏVE REALISM

Naïve realism is a psychological theory about how people perceive their own perceptions. At its core, naïve realism posits that (1) we believe that we see the world objectively and without bias, (2) we expect that others will come to the same conclusions as we do if they are exposed to the same information and are processing it rationally, and (3) if others disagree with us, we assume they are uninformed, irrational, or biased.[1]

In other words, naïve realism suggests that individuals believe their perception of the world reflects the world "as it really is," and if others see things differently, it must be due to a flaw in their perception or reasoning. This can lead to misunderstandings and conflicts, as people often overestimate the degree to which their subjective perspectives are "correct" or "objective."

Imagine you're at the annual family dinner, sitting around the table, engaged in conversation with your loved ones. Suddenly, a debate ensues on a controversial topic. You see Aunt Martha on one side of the argument and Cousin Bob on the other, each fervently stating their point of view. Both are equally convinced of the correctness of their perspective, and neither seems willing to budge. This argument could be about politics, parenting, or pineapple on pizza; it doesn't really matter. What matters is that they're not just expressing their opinions, they are sharing their lived experiences, their backgrounds, and the various factors that have shaped their perceptions.

This is where the concept of naïve realism comes into play. Aunt Martha and Cousin Bob, like many of us, may unconsciously believe that their individual view of the world is the unvarnished truth. Each thinks, *I see things as they are. If only others could see "reality" as clearly as I do, they would agree with me.* This viewpoint suggests an egocentric bias—an overreliance on their personal perspective, leading them to dismiss or underestimate the perspectives of others.

Let's imagine Aunt Martha grew up in a strict household and believes in discipline, while Cousin Bob, having been raised in a freer environment, values personal freedom. Their upbringing, their personal experiences, their joys and heartaches all play into how they perceive the topic at hand. Yet the illusion of naïve realism might lead them to forget these differences, and rather than understanding the other's viewpoint, they might dismiss it as simply "wrong."

But what if we could challenge this naïve realism? What if we could remind ourselves that our perspectives, while valid to us, are just that—perspectives. They are not an absolute reflection of reality, but a collage of our experiences, cultural identities, and emotional states. Reminding ourselves of how our experiences have impacted us might help us embrace a broader understanding of the world around us, accept the validity of differing views, and expand our worldview. What if, instead of judgment, we brought with us a curious mindset and wondered where the person might be coming from or what they might have experienced to led them to their conclusion?

Let's be real here: this can be exhausting. There are days when we're emotionally drained and the last thing we want is a deep philosophical debate about the nature of perception. That's okay, too. It's crucial to take care of our emotional health and pick our deep dives wisely. Sometimes we need a break to have healthy conversations. When a conversation is moving to a place of disrespect, we might consider taking a deep breath, taking a break, and possibly pausing the conversation to move it from an overheated tone to a relatively calm (while still passionate) one. Nevertheless, on the days when we're up for it, pushing past the limitations of naïve realism can lead to richer discussions, deeper connections, and a more nuanced understanding of the world we live in. In order to have conversations like this, first we need to feel safe doing so.

PSYCHOLOGICAL SAFETY

In every corner of the globe, you can find offices where silence, not dialogue, is the chosen tool of communication.

Employees walk on eggshells, opting for a smile and a nod over sharing their genuine views, their deep-rooted concerns, or a potentially transformative idea. It's as though we've been programmed to favor the apparent tranquility of agreement over the risk of ruffling feathers.

The echo chambers thus created are not only stifling but also detrimental to the company's progress and the well-being of its workforce. Research suggests that emotional intelligence plays a pivotal role in navigating the tumultuous waters of conflict resolution; hence, organizations can truly flourish when they foster environments where diverse opinions can be shared freely and openly, always with an underlying foundation of respect.[2] I believe the same can be true for our homes and our communities.

Yet it's undeniable: not all of us are equipped or feel prepared to dive headfirst into challenging dialogues every single day. Sometimes, our emotional reservoirs run dry. I vividly recall the aftermath of George Floyd's tragic death. Friends, knowing my passion for inclusivity and belonging, reached out for insight, for understanding. I had to draw boundaries, to allow myself a time to process my emotions. I prayed, cried, talked it over with close friends, and allowed myself to feel. Only then could I ensure that my responses weren't born from frustration, but from a deep-seated desire to constructively further the conversation. I was better prepared to have honest conversations, because I had a support system I could rely on to process what occurred.

Does this resonate with you? Do you find yourself shying away from difficult conversations, fearing they're land mines in your path? I want you to feel confident, not cornered, in these scenarios. We have a better chance of having respectful disagreements when we are aware and taking care of ourselves. Also, know that when others don't feel safe, they will struggle to respectfully disagree. My aim, as we move into the next chapter and beyond, is to provide you with practical tools to engage, navigate, and even instigate these pivotal discussions. Let's choose to be honest, open, and understanding communicators in this place we call the world!

REFLECTIONS AND ACTIONS

1. What did disagreement look like for you growing up (both positive and negative) and how has it impacted how you disagree today?

2. Can you pinpoint a pivotal moment in your life that has profoundly influenced your perspective on disagreement? This reflective question isn't just about identifying that moment but understanding its enduring impact on you.

3. Is there someone in your life, a person you're embroiled in inner conflict with, whom you need to forgive? Much like my experience with forgiving my brother, you may find that unresolved conflicts are rooted in the rocky soil of unforgiveness. Let me clarify that forgiveness isn't necessarily about reconciliation; it's more about liberating yourself to move forward. This might be a crucial step toward progress.

CHAPTER 4

The Disagreement Divide

*Are You Building Up Barriers
or Bridging the Divide?*

This chapter explores the divide that exists between "you" and "them" and gives you practical tools to bridge that divide rather than build up barriers. This will be the introduction to the 5 Pillars of Bridging the Divide. In this chapter, pay attention to ways to set helpful boundaries as you engage the disagreement divide.

Imagine stepping back in time to the early 1990s. South Africa is in turmoil, a tinderbox of racial tension primed to explode at any moment. Enter Nelson Mandela, a man just released from a twenty-seven-year stint in jail, not for theft, not for violence, but for standing against apartheid. His challenge? To steer this stormy sea of discord toward the shores of unity and democracy. An insurmountable task? Perhaps for most, but not for Mandela.

In the nineties, South Africa was a jigsaw puzzle with pieces forced into wrong places. Mandela's African National Congress (ANC) was at loggerheads with the apartheid-supporting

National Party and other factions like the Zulu nationalist Inkatha Freedom Party. But their battlefield was not limited to courtrooms and political debates. This was raw and brutal, often culminating in a crimson tide of violence.

Yet, amidst this chaotic landscape, Mandela stood tall, an unwavering beacon of peace. The high-pressure negotiations weren't just another political game for him, they were the crucible to forge a new South Africa. Mandela wasn't interested in the short game, in merely winning an argument. His eyes were set on a greater prize—healing a fractured nation.

Mandela was not a steamroller, flattening opposition. Instead, he was a *bridge-builder*. His approach was one of deep listening, acknowledging the fears and concerns of his adversaries, understanding their point of view, and then weaving a tapestry of compromise where everyone could see their threads.

To grasp the essence of Mandela's diplomacy, let's revisit 1992. The Boipatong massacre had just occurred, a horrifying incident where forty-five lives were lost in a racial clash. Mandela could have slammed his fists on the table and stormed out of the negotiations. But he didn't. He channeled this tragedy into a potent reminder of the dire need to end apartheid and foster a peaceful South Africa.

And the extraordinary thing is, Mandela's patience, empathy, and resilience paid off. His navigation through the tumultuous waters of discord led to the landmark Interim Constitution of 1993 and the first democratic, nonracial elections in 1994. This remarkable man, who bore the weight of imprisonment for almost three decades, was then chosen to serve as the first Black president of South Africa.

So yes, Nelson Mandela, the epitome of perseverance, was indeed a master at dealing with disagreements. His life stands as testament to the idea that it's not about vanquishing an adversary, but finding common ground and creating a shared future. It's a legacy worth remembering, cherishing, and applying in our own lives. Because, in the end, it's about understanding that disagreements, whether on a national stage or a personal level, can be bridges to unity, not chasms of division.

SEEING THE "OTHER"

Imagine a world where we can disagree passionately yet still foster an atmosphere of profound respect. By challenging the disagreement divide, we can do just that. Picture each of us on opposing cliffs, separated by a cavernous divide of differing beliefs and perspectives. In this divide, we have two essential tools at our disposal—barriers or bridges.

When we choose to dehumanize those we differ with, each derogatory word, each dismissive action, becomes a barrier. These barriers close us off from each other, erecting a wall that fosters division, hostility, and misunderstanding. Our views become echo chambers, devoid of growth and learning.

On the other hand, when we decide to humanize our counterparts, to respect their inherent worth as fellow travelers on this planet, we lay the foundation to build a bridge. Remember, the act of bridge-building doesn't imply that we must adopt their perspectives or they ours; it's about acknowledging and engaging with the thread of humanity that weaves us together.

Bridging the disagreement divide focuses on five pillars that form the very core of this philosophy, guiding us to sustain respect and understanding amidst conflicts. It's about engaging with people in a way that is not just tolerant but also accepting, affirming, and enriching of who they are even if we never accept, affirm, or are enriched by what they believe.

My vision is a world where we all can safely disagree, yet still see and value the human being on the other side of the argument. It's not about giving up your truth but understanding that others have their truth, too, no matter how misguided you think they might be. Within this understanding, we cultivate a shared respect that transcends disagreement. It's possible. It's achievable. By embracing the 5 Pillars of Bridging the Divide, we can step forward and create a world where respect amid disagreements becomes the norm, rather than the exception.

Part II will discuss the pillars in more detail along with practical actions to live them on an everyday basis. For now, here's a brief summary of each:

PILLAR 1: CHALLENGE YOUR PERSPECTIVE
Frame your perspective for more humanization and less dehumanization. This pillar emphasizes the importance of viewing others as fellow human beings with their own unique experiences and perspectives, rather than demonizing them for having different beliefs. It encourages empathetic understanding and respectful dialogue, promoting a shift in perspective from viewing the "other" as an adversary to seeing them as a partner in conversation.

PILLAR 2: BE THE STUDENT Focus on learning, not lecturing. This pillar prioritizes active learning and listening over unidirectional communication or preaching. It involves setting aside personal biases and preconceived notions to truly understand and appreciate the perspectives of others. This shift from lecture-oriented to learning-oriented communication promotes mutual respect and understanding.

PILLAR 3: CULTIVATE YOUR CURIOSITY Fill the gaps in your understanding with curiosity, not conclusions. This pillar encourages individuals to approach gaps in their knowledge with curiosity and a desire to learn, rather than jumping to conclusions. It values the practice of asking questions, seeking answers, and being open to new information rather than forming judgments based on incomplete information. It promotes a mindset of continuous learning and growth.

PILLAR 4: SEEK THE GRAY Find the gray in your inter-actions with others. This pillar emphasizes the importance of seeking common ground and collaborative solutions, rather than thinking in terms of absolutes or black and white. It recognizes that real-world problems often exist in the gray areas and require nuanced, collaborative, and multidimensional solutions that respect the diversity of perspectives involved.

PILLAR 5: AGREE TO RESPECT Formulate and act on your plan to humanize and not harm. This final pillar underscores the importance of fostering genuine con-nections with others and prioritizing actions that uphold the dignity and humanity of all parties involved. It means creating plans and strategies that focus on humanizing others, rather than causing harm or escalating conflicts. It promotes a culture of peace, understanding, and unity, while respecting the uniqueness and individuality of each person.

As shared in chapter 1, my team and I have found in our research that each of these pillars has a counterpart, a response that builds up a barrier instead of a bridge (see table 4-1). In other words, you have a choice to either bridge

TABLE 4-1: Bridging the Divide or Building Up Barriers

	BRIDGING THE DIVIDE	BUILDING UP BARRIERS
Pillar 1	Challenge Your Perspective	Close Off Other Perspectives
Pillar 2	Be the Student	Assert Your Authority Only
Pillar 3	Cultivate Your Curiosity	Coast to Conclusions
Pillar 4	Seek the Gray	See Only the Black and White
Pillar 5	Agree to Respect	Disrespectfully (Dis)Agree

the divide, which leads to respectful disagreement, or build a barrier, which leads to disrespectful (dis)agreement.

Amy and Bill

In the heart of a small midwestern town in the US, two individuals came to represent the divisiveness that seemed to grip not only their community but the nation as a whole. On one side was Amy, an outspoken liberal and organizer for various social justice movements. On the other was Bill, a staunch conservative and owner of the local gun store. Despite living in the same town for decades, they had found themselves on opposite sides of every local and national debate, from climate change to gun control, and their disagreements were often public and heated.

One year, a controversial bill was passed in their state, and tensions escalated to an all-time high. The town was divided, with sides forming around Amy and Bill. Protests and counterprotests sprung up, creating a palpable tension that permeated everyday life.

It was around this time that Bill's wife fell seriously ill. With the town divided and tensions high, there was little room for empathy or understanding. Bill, engrossed in managing his wife's healthcare, maintaining his business, and keeping up with the local disputes, found himself overwhelmed.

It was then that Amy made a choice. Despite their differences, she realized that she and Bill shared a common humanity. She decided to bridge the divide, at least on a personal level. Amy reached out to Bill, offering to set up a local fundraiser to help with his wife's medical bills.

Bill, surprised but touched, agreed. During the fundraiser, the two found themselves talking, really talking, for the first time. They spoke about their fears, hopes, and dreams. They spoke about their town and its future. They found that they both loved their community deeply, even if they had different ideas of what was best for it.

This act of empathy and understanding did not resolve all their disagreements, of course, but it did spark a change. In their subsequent public debates, their language was less fiery, their attacks less personal. They encouraged their supporters to engage in civil discourse rather than hateful rhetoric. They began working together on community projects where their goals aligned, such as improving local schools and parks.

Amy and Bill's story rippled through their community. People began to remember that their neighbors were not faceless enemies but individuals with their own struggles and stories. Conversations began to happen, slowly bridging the divide that had formed in the town.

Amy's small act of kindness toward Bill did not erase the complexities and challenges of their differing viewpoints, but it did humanize the "other side," fostering a spirit of understanding and dialogue. Amy's choice to reach out in a time of personal crisis, and Bill humbly accepting Amy's help, marked the beginning of a shift in their community—a shift from division to unity, from hostility to dialogue. It was a powerful reminder that even amidst deep disagreements, there is room for empathy and understanding.

Amy is a beacon of patience and understanding in this story. It would have been all too easy for her to build up barriers, but instead, she chose to engage with Bill's humanity. You might be wondering why Amy had to be the one to reach out, but that misses the point. You could easily reverse the names, and the lesson remains the same: we *all* have the power to choose to bridge the divide or build up barriers.

There's a necessary balance, however. There are moments when amplifying our boundaries is crucial to maintain respect and love for those we hold dear.

THE IMPORTANCE OF BOUNDARIES

Boundaries in disagreements serve as pivotal guidelines to ensure that discussions remain respectful, productive, and focused. Just as fences demarcate property lines, establishing clear boundaries during conflicts delineates what behaviors are acceptable and which are not. These boundaries prevent conversations from devolving into personal attacks, preserve the integrity of the discourse, and enable participants to engage with differing viewpoints without fear of overstepping or causing unintentional harm. By setting such standards, individuals can approach disagreements with a mutual understanding, making them more likely to reach a constructive resolution rather than escalating tension.

Darcie and Her Dad

Take Darcie, a dear friend of mine, who beautifully demonstrates this delicate balance. Darcie has found a way to humanize her dad, and it lies in a simple yet powerful act: she's set a boundary to no longer discuss politics when she visits. She listened to his views countless times, grasped his perspective, and often still disagreed. When she would oppose her dad's views, he would respond with hostile comments like "That's a stupid perspective." Instead of choosing to disengage (as she initially wanted to do), Darcie has opted to enjoy her father's company by simply steering clear of political debates and communicating to her dad that she prefers not to talk politics when she visits throughout the year. She instead wants to go over her fond memories of growing up and relive some of the best moments of their epic camping adventures together.

You see, boundaries can serve as our compass, guiding us through the rugged terrain of disagreements. Some are temporary waypoints, while others remain fixed landmarks. And if you find yourself struggling in setting these boundaries, remember, it's okay to seek help. Friends and, more importantly, trained therapists can provide invaluable guidance to help you understand when to assert yourself and when to persist in the face of discomfort. Boundaries are crucial in respectful disagreements for several reasons:[1]

- **Preserving respect.** By setting limits, we can ensure that a conversation doesn't devolve into personal attacks, insults, or other forms of disrespect. Boundaries help to keep discussions focused on the issue at hand, not on the personal attributes of the people involved.

- **Providing emotional safety.** Boundaries can provide emotional safety by protecting individuals from feeling overwhelmed, attacked, or hurt. This safety allows for more open and honest communication.

- **Encouraging constructive dialogue.** When boundaries are set and respected, discussions are more likely to remain productive and solutions-oriented, rather than devolving into unproductive, hurtful arguments.

- **Fostering mutual understanding.** When each party respects the boundaries of the other, it shows a mutual understanding and appreciation for each other's perspectives. It shows that both parties are committed to hearing and understanding each other.

- **Preventing escalation.** Boundaries can help prevent disagreements from escalating into heated arguments or conflicts, which can harm relationships. They serve as a reminder to maintain self-control and to respect the rights and feelings of the other party.

- **Maintaining focus.** Boundaries help keep the discussion on the topic at hand and avoid irrelevant or harmful digressions, which can divert the conversation from its purpose and hinder the resolution process.

- **Enhancing relationships.** By maintaining respectful boundaries, individuals show that they value the relationship above the disagreement, which can strengthen their bond and foster trust.

Setting boundaries in disagreements allows for healthier, more respectful, and more productive communication, which can lead to a deeper understanding and more effective problem-solving. Boundary setting is a part of bridging the divide, because the goal is the same: to find the best way to humanize the other person. While boundary setting may look like a barrier to some, it's the intent that matters the most. For example, if you notice the disagreement veering into personal attacks, you can set a boundary to take a temporary pause from the disagreement and come back to it only when you're both able to communicate free of personal attacks.

For example, I had a friend who would only communicate negative feedback to me through text or email, and it annoyed me greatly. I took time to ask her why she did this and to also explain that I don't prefer to receive negative feedback this way. She continued to share her negative feedback through text and email, and I gave her a gracious warning that I preferred to not communicate this way. She continued to do it, and I chose to move on from that friendship. Boundary setting isn't always "nice," but it can be helpful in enforcing honest conversations with each other.

How to Set Clear Boundaries

Setting boundaries is a crucial skill set that can help us bridge the divide with our ideological other. Without clear boundaries, we sometimes wade into the waters of disrespect and hurt relationships in the process.

Elena and Raj

Elena and Raj were both seasoned developers in the tech department of a thriving startup. Their programming skills were unmatched, but their approaches were polar opposites. Elena, methodical and precise, believed in extensive planning. Raj, on the other hand, was a firm advocate of rapid prototyping, believing that errors could be fixed as they went along.

One day, the duo was tasked with leading a crucial project that could define the company's future. From the outset, their differing philosophies sparked friction. Raj wanted to dive in, confident they could troubleshoot on the fly, while

Elena insisted on mapping out every detail before writing a single line of code.

Realizing they were on the brink of a major fallout, Elena took a deep breath and suggested, "Raj, how about we set some boundaries for this discussion? I truly value your approach, but we need to find a middle ground."

Raj nodded. "I appreciate that, Elena. Let's agree not to interrupt each other and ensure our critiques are about the process, not personal."

Elena smiled. "I'd also like to suggest that if either of us feels overwhelmed, we take a short break. What do you think?"

"That sounds fair," Raj responded.

With these boundaries in place, they began to dissect each other's methodologies. They found that Elena's detailed planning could predict and avoid major pitfalls, but Raj's rapid prototyping could adapt to unexpected challenges, making the development more agile.

To their surprise, the respectful exchange opened their eyes to a hybrid approach. Elena's planning ensured the project's backbone was solid, while Raj's adaptive strategies allowed for flexibility.

The result? Their project was a massive success, and the company reaped the benefits. Not only did Elena and Raj deliver, but they also set an example for their peers. Their disagreement, steered by mutual respect and clear boundaries, had forged an innovation neither had seen coming.

From that day, the tale of their collaboration became legendary in the company corridors—not as a story of conflict, but as a testament to the magic that happens when two differing minds come together with respect. If only we were able to tie up all challenging situations like this, but life and people are messy.

Ten Tips for Boundary Setting

Setting boundaries for respectful disagreement is essential for maintaining healthy interpersonal relationships, whether in a professional setting or in your personal life. Here are ten simple tips to guide you in this process:[2]

- **Practice self-awareness and reflection.** Before engaging in a discussion, recognize your own triggers and sensitivities. Understanding what upsets you can help you communicate your boundaries more effectively.

- **Communicate openly.** Clearly and calmly express your needs and boundaries at the start of a conversation. For instance, "I'd like for us to have this discussion, but I'd appreciate it if we avoid raising our voices."

- **Use "I" statements.** Frame your boundaries in a way that communicates your feelings and needs without blaming or accusing the other person. For example, "I feel disrespected when interrupted" rather than "You always interrupt me."

- **Actively listen.** Make an effort to truly understand the other person's perspective. This shows respect and can also help you recognize their boundaries.

- **Avoid personal attacks.** Stick to the topic at hand and avoid bringing in unrelated issues or making personal jabs.

- **Set time limits.** If the topic is heated, consider setting a time limit for discussion. This can prevent exhaustion and reduce the chances of the conversation spiraling.

- **Take breaks when needed.** If the discussion becomes too intense, it's okay to suggest taking a break and returning to the topic later. This allows both parties to cool down and gather their thoughts.

◘ **Reiterate boundaries if crossed.** If you feel your boundaries are being violated during the discussion, calmly and firmly remind the other person of them.

◘ **Seek mediation.** In cases where an agreement seems impossible, consider bringing in a neutral third party to mediate the discussion.

◘ **Reflect and adjust.** After the discussion, take some time to reflect on what went well and what could be improved. Adjust your boundaries as needed for future conversations.

Remember, the primary aim of setting boundaries isn't to win an argument but to ensure that disagreements are productive and respectful and lead to mutual understanding. One of the most important tasks here, and often one of the most difficult, is determining when you need to set a boundary or challenge yourself to have more patience and understanding.

Boundaries or More Patience?

Distinguishing between the need to set a boundary and the need for more patience and understanding during a disagreement can be challenging, and often requires introspection, empathy, and an understanding of the context. The nature of the disagreement often provides the first clue. When disagreements involve personal attacks, insults, or any form of disrespect, it's a clear sign that you need to set boundaries. On the other hand, differences in opinion or simple misunderstandings might require more patience and a desire to seek clarity. Your personal feelings and reactions also serve as indicators. Feeling emotionally or physically unsafe or consistently drained after interactions points to a need for boundary setting. However, if your frustration stems from not seeing eye-to-eye or from the conversation taking longer than you anticipated, this might be a chance to demonstrate patience.

Repetition and established patterns in behavior can also guide your response. Continuous harmful behaviors, despite being addressed, call for clearer boundaries, while isolated incidents or genuine struggles on the other person's part might benefit from a more understanding approach. It's also crucial to weigh intent against impact. Regardless of someone's good intentions, if their actions have a detrimental impact, setting boundaries is valid. But when miscommunication is at play and their intentions seem genuine, it can be worthwhile to take some time to explain perspectives and seek mutual understanding.

Your emotional energy and capacity in the moment can't be overlooked. Emotional exhaustion or vulnerability might necessitate boundary setting, while having the emotional bandwidth could be an opportunity to navigate the disagreement with patience. Lastly, the history and nature of the relationship play a role. Individuals with a history of overstepping or strained relationships need clear boundaries for preservation, while first-time disagreements or those with close, trusted individuals might benefit more from patience and understanding. Often, the best approach combines both: setting clear boundaries about the manner of communication while being patient about the content of the disagreement. While there's not a one-size-fits-all, clear-cut way to determine what to do, you should always (1) check in with yourself about how you are feeling/thinking, (2) check in with the other person, and (3) choose respect, no matter what. Sometimes the most respectful thing we can do for ourselves and others is to set a boundary.

Throughout the next chapters, we'll delve deeper into each pillar that supports bridging the disagreement divide, and I'll guide you on how to put the pillars into practice to ensure you're building more bridges than barriers. Remember, although we won't always find that magical middle ground where both parties fully meet each other, every step we take toward humanizing and respecting the "other" is a step toward a more empathetic, understanding world.

REFLECTIONS AND ACTIONS

1. Which of the 5 Pillars is a strength for you and which is an area for more growth? Why do you think that is?

2. Which of the ten steps for setting boundaries do you already do well and which do you currently struggle with the most?

3. What is one relationship in your life that could benefit from setting a healthy boundary? Set a time to share graciously and assertively.

The 5 Pillars of Bridging the Divide

The time for the healing of the wounds has come. The moment to bridge the chasms that divide us has come. The time to build is upon us.

—NELSON MANDELA

In part II we'll explore each of the 5 Pillars in detail. Chapter 5 will help you challenge your perspectives to better understand those of others. Chapter 6 will remind you of the need to always be a student and focus on learning and lecturing. In chapter 7, you'll learn to reignite your curiosity as you engage others. Chapter 8 will encourage you to find the common (not always middle) ground in an effort to move away from a purely black-or-white viewpoint. Chapter 9 will focus on helping you acknowledge others and choose to respect them. We'll end with chapter 10, where I'll help you move forward and get started in doing the important work of respectfully disagreeing.

The 5 Pillars of Bridging the Divide model, shown in figure 2, helps us bridge the disagreement divide (the space between you and "them"), not always by changing what we believe but rather by learning to appreciate others' humanity.

The 5 Pillars
of Bridging the Divide

1	2	3	4	5
CHALLENGE YOUR PERSPECTIVE	**BE THE STUDENT**	**CULTIVATE YOUR CURIOSITY**	**SEEK THE GRAY**	**AGREE TO RESPECT**
Position yourself to actively seek out alternative viewpoints and question long-held assumptions for more humanization	Focus on learning and not lecturing by adopting a mindset of constant learning and personal growth	Fill in the gaps with curiosity and not conclusions by asking meaningful questions and exploring the unknown	Search for the gray within the black and white to create better dialogue in a nuanced and ambiguous world	Formulate and act on your plan to respect and not harm others in order to build a bridge of deeper understanding

YOU

THEM

The Disagreement Divide

FIGURE 2: The 5 Pillars of Bridging the Divide

CHAPTER 5

How You See Is What You Get

Pillar 1, Challenge Your Perspective

This chapter focuses on how we can choose to humanize others, open ourselves to better understand others' perspective, and deal with what stops us from doing so. I'll help you identify a few ways you can improve in humanizing your ideological other.

Picture this: It's 1968, and two curious researchers, Robert Rosenthal and Lenore Jacobson, step into a lively public elementary school in south San Francisco. They carry with them a burning question: How much does what a teacher expect of a student influence how that student performs?[1]

To start, they test the students' IQs, but they keep the results a secret. They come up with an interesting experimental strategy. They randomly select about one in five students across all grades and tell their teachers, "Watch these kids closely—they're late bloomers!" They spin a story, saying that these students are about to hit an intellectual growth spurt and make leaps and bounds in their academic performance in the coming year.

Of course, this was all just a bit of make-believe. These students were chosen by chance, not because of any stand-out results in the initial IQ tests.

Rosenthal and Jacobson had a hunch that if teachers believed these students were destined for greatness, the students would rise to meet those expectations. The researchers thought teachers would unknowingly start to act differently toward these students, giving them more opportunities, more feedback, and ultimately nudging them toward better performance.

Fast-forward to the end of the school year. The researchers test the students' IQs again. Lo and behold, those who were labeled "late bloomers" indeed bloomed. They showed a significant growth in their IQ scores compared to their classmates who were not labeled late bloomers or as gifted at all, for that matter. It was a fascinating discovery—the power of belief had transformed these ordinary students into high achievers.

This surprising result was dubbed the "Pygmalion Effect," inspired by a Greek myth about the sculptor Pygmalion, who fell in love with a statue he carved, which then magically came to life. The message was clear: expectations can be powerful, and they can coax out great performance where we might not expect it.

Now, no study is perfect, and this one had its fair share of critics. Some raised eyebrows at the methodology or doubted the reliability of the IQ tests used. But even with these critiques, the core idea—that our perceptions and expectations can shape the world around us—has been echoed in studies across many fields, far beyond just education. After all, isn't that a story we can all relate to?

How the teachers saw their students impacted what happened with those students. I believe these same principles can carry over to our disagreements as well. How we see the people we disagree with or our ideological "others" will shape how we interact with them. One approach that I share during my team's learning experiences (and practice myself) is to talk to yourself. I know, I know, I didn't think it would work either, because I'm not known to be an affirmations-type person, but what I found in the research surprised me. Positive self-talk can favorably impact how we show up for ourselves and in disagreements.[2] This also relates to much of the brain research on cognitive reframing and how it can shape how we see ourselves and others.[3] Before and during disagreements, consider doing what I try my best to do—tell yourself that the person you're engaging is your equal, worthy of dignity, value, and respect. If it is a person you love, value, and trust, you can also remind yourself that they truly have your best interests in mind and are not out to intentionally hurt you. These small actions over time can have a profound impact on your conversations and how you disagree.

THE POWER OF CHOICE—
SEEING OTHERS THROUGH A NEW LENS

At the core of our existence lies the beautiful gift of choice—an attribute that forms the backbone of human resilience and evolution. It underscores the premise that no matter what happened in our past, we have the opportunity to choose how we move forward, focusing on hope rather than despair. This may be harder for some than for others, but it is always a choice.

When we encounter others, the first notion that should ground our thoughts is Pillar 1—the recognition that every individual we come across is a distinct entity with personal desires, dreams, and concerns who deserves our utmost respect, dignity, and value. Each person is more than their words and actions; they are complex beings full of aspirations, doubts, emotions, and experiences that shape their worldviews. To state it simply: they are humans!

Pillar 1, Challenge Your Perspective, forms the mental groundwork before any interaction takes place. It requires that we see others as equal humans, as deserving of compassion and understanding as we are. It forms the cornerstone upon which our understanding of others can be built.

We've all heard the saying, "What you see is what you get," but what if we amended that to "How you see is what you get"? This small but potent shift can be transformative. Our perceptions, thoughts, and beliefs largely define our realities and experiences. This is our choice.

Our beliefs are often the mirror images of the perspectives and opinions of others—be it friends, family, experts, or online users. But what if we consciously decide to alter this dynamic? What if we empower ourselves to shape our beliefs not just based on the influence of others, but on our own discernment, understanding, and empathy?

That brings us to the critical choice between our "course" and our "captivity." To have a course is to map out our path, to embody hope, and to envision a way forward. In contrast, being captive signifies surrendering to external pressures, feeling confined to whatever life throws at us.

Let me share a story from an experience at the airport. It was a day like any other until a passenger erupted in rage over a delayed flight. He blamed everyone in sight—from airline staff to security personnel—yet he overlooked the storm that had *actually* delayed the flight, something no one had control over. Instead of taking ownership of his response to the situation, he chose to toss blame, trapping himself in his own emotional captivity. That passenger was me. It was a moment I am not proud of, and I shudder when I recall it. I now choose to thank the agents for their hard work (yes, even when they close the door to the plane I am running frantically to catch). After all, it's not their fault, and it's my choice how I respond in that situation.

By acknowledging that we have a choice in our responses and how we view others, we liberate ourselves from this self-imposed confinement. The beauty of this power is that it allows us to see others not just as carriers of opinions and ideas, but as fellow humans navigating the complex tapestry of life.

The power of choice is, therefore, not just about choosing our actions, but about choosing our perspectives, our responses, and ultimately, our own evolution. It is a testament to our capacity for change, growth, and understanding—and *it begins with how we choose to see others and how we frame them.* Are we ultimately willing to allow our perspective to be challenged to see both ourselves and others differently?

COGNITIVE REFRAMING AND SELF

Cognitive reframing, a concept that comes from psychology and neuroscience, is like being the director of the movie that is your mind. Imagine you're cruising along the highway of life when suddenly, you find yourself caught in a traffic jam of negative thoughts. Sentiments like *I'm just not good enough* and *I always mess things up* blare like horns, overwhelming the soundtrack of your day. In such moments, cognitive reframing can be your directorial call to "cut!" It helps you pause, view the situation from multiple angles, and reshoot the scene with a more positive and empowering script.

Consider an everyday situation where cognitive reframing can come into play. Imagine you tried out a new dinner recipe, but the results were less than appetizing. Your first reaction might be, *I'm a terrible cook. I can't do anything right.* That's the script your mind automatically adheres to. However, cognitive reframing empowers you to call "cut!" on this narrative, hit the rewind button, and reassess the situation from a fresh perspective.

Instead of marinating in the "I'm a terrible cook" narrative, you're encouraged to consider alternative possibilities. The recipe might have been more complex than you realized, or maybe you missed a step while multitasking. The reshoot of your internal dialogue could then be: *This recipe didn't turn out as expected, but it was pretty complex. I'll try a simpler dish next time or make sure I stay focused while cooking.*

The goal isn't to gloss over failures or negative experiences, but to challenge unhelpful or overly negative thoughts. Cognitive reframing helps us become kinder, more understanding directors of our life's narrative. It's about reshaping our view of personal challenges, setbacks, and even the way we perceive others. By doing so, we open the door to optimism, resilience, and a more empowered approach to life. This is important to the idea of respectfully disagreeing, because when we see ourselves in a healthy way it allows us to enter conversations without trying to overcompensate based on what we think or feel. Some people have found gratitude journals, or journaling in general, helpful to practice cognitive reframing. Ask yourself how you can view your situation differently.

I have also seen cognitive reframing in play when we operate from a place of superiority. When I used to rent cars quite a bit, I would rent a convertible because I loved putting the top down. I would pull up to the stoplight with the wind flowing through my hair (yeah, I am still bald), look at the car stopped next to me, and nod with an internal feeling of being "better than." I noticed that I did this one too many times and I challenged my thought process. I began saying to myself, *Justin, this is a rental car, and not only that but you aren't better (or worse) than them because of the car you drive.* Where might you feel superior to others is where a little corrective cognitive reframing can be beneficial. Not only can it help you move out of the areas where you're feeling superior to others, but it also promotes the self-awareness you need to check yourself when engaging others.

COGNITIVE REFRAMING AND OTHERS

The power of cognitive reframing isn't just for changing our personal outlook—it's like a secret weapon we can use to improve our relationships, too. We've all been in situations where we make snap judgments about people. Maybe it's because of biases we didn't even know we had, or past experiences that are clouding our view, or assumptions we've jumped to without realizing it. But here's where cognitive reframing comes into play—it's like a mental pause button that encourages us to stop, step back, and reconsider our initial impressions.[4]

Imagine meeting someone who seems standoffish or aloof. Your gut reaction might be to label them "unfriendly" and move on. But cognitive reframing is like a mental nudge that encourages us to dig a little deeper and think about other possibilities. Maybe this person is just having one of those days, or maybe they're introverted and recharging internally.

Or say you've sent a message to a friend and they don't respond right away. It's easy to think they're ignoring you or that they're not interested in your friendship. But with cognitive reframing, we can switch gears and come up with other explanations. Maybe they're swamped at work, or maybe they saw your message and then got distracted by something else.

The best part about using cognitive reframing in our relationships is that it helps us avoid jumping to conclusions and instead allows us to cultivate empathy and understanding. It's a reminder that everyone is on their own unique journey with their own trials and tribulations. This mindset can lead to more positive, patient, and empathetic relationships, making our lives—and the lives of those around us—just a little bit better. It's one of the reasons I love the book *What Happened to You?* This book challenges the popular idea of "What's wrong with you?" by asking us to look deeper into the people we encounter and the experiences that have shaped who they are today.[5]

Now, the tricky part about reframing is catching those negative thoughts in the first place, but this is the first step.[6] You'd be surprised at how sneaky they can be! For instance, I was at the gym the other day, chatting with one of the trainers and another gym-goer. The trainer was venting about a client who threw a fit because he couldn't use the bikes in a private room anymore. As they told the story, I initially got very irritated by this "entitled" person, too, but I took a mental pause and asked myself (yep, I talk to myself) if there was another way to look at this.

I tried to see things from the client's perspective and suggested that maybe he was just upset about the change in his routine. By the end of chat, even though we agreed that the client shouldn't have lashed out, I think we had a better understanding of how he might have arrived at his reaction. It's amazing how much easier it is to do this when we're looking at someone else's situation, rather than our own—but it's definitely doable!

And you know what else? The stories we create about others can be hugely influenced by who we consider to be part of our "circles of grace"—our closest friends, family, or those we feel most connected to. For those within our in-group, we're more likely to make excuses for their behavior, while for those outside, we might be more likely to judge harshly. It's like when someone cuts you off in traffic—do you instantly think *How rude! They must be texting!* or do you consider that they might be dealing with an emergency? The stories we create in our heads can have a big impact, especially if we don't take the time to question them. The great news is that we have the power to change those stories, if we *choose* to, and this will help us have better conversations.

While reframing can help us change how we see, it's still important to expose ourselves to seeing different things. Let's take a look at how.

SELECTIVE EXPOSURE

Selective exposure, also known as *congeniality bias* or *confirmation bias*, is "a theory within the practice of psychology . . . that historically refers to individuals' tendency to favor information which reinforces their pre-existing views while avoiding contradictory information."[7] Think about your morning coffee run. More often than not, you go for your regular, familiar choice—a caramel latte with almond milk, perhaps. Sometimes you might try a different drink, but generally you go for the ones you're pretty sure you'll like. As with your beverage of choice, you might lean toward consuming information that you're comfortable with or that aligns with your established beliefs, especially those close to your heart. You might expose yourself to contrasting views, but often they're the ones you find easy to dispute. Like your favorite coffee shop, your perspective is cozy and familiar, making you feel like you're in the right place.[8]

Selective exposure also shows up when we choose where to sit at a training. We might briefly scan the room for "our tribe," or people we think are the most like us. It shows up when we choose what news programs to watch on TV, and what social media messages we choose to engage with.

Think of navigating your world as moving through a well-curated music playlist. You enjoy the songs that resonate with your mood, skipping those that don't quite fit. Selective exposure works like the "skip" button on our playlist, keeping us in a bubble of agreeable ideas. When faced with an "out-of-tune" idea, our knee-jerk reaction isn't to adjust our preferences but to blame the song for being "bad."

While exposing ourselves to difference is an important aspect of respectfully disagreeing, it's not the end goal. "Simply choosing to engage with opposing views may not lead to greater understanding or cooperation if the language of that engagement is unreceptive. . . . The linguistic behavior that people exhibit in conversation can powerfully affect their partners' perceptions, engagement, and willingness to cooperate with them."[9] It's not merely the act of discussing your differing opinions that matters, but how you approach the conversation. The tone and words you use can significantly impact the other person's perceptions and willingness to engage with you. Are your language and tone condemning or curious? Do you say, "Why would you believe in something like that?" or "Tell me more about how you came to that belief." What you say and how you say it matters in respectful disagreement. People are less likely to engage if they feel unsafe or attacked with yelling and abusive language.

Consider this scenario: you're an adventure lover, but while researching for an upcoming trip, you skip certain treks because you believe they're too strenuous for you. This is similar to how we, driven by selective exposure, tend to avoid discussions or people challenging our views. I've noticed this behavior in myself, too. As a self-proclaimed centrist, I found myself sidestepping specific news outlets during my research on this book, a step that was neither completely rational nor beneficial. When I leaned into watching news channels that were more in line with either the "left" or the "right," neither was as bad as I had imagined it to be. This didn't mean that I agreed with everything I read or watched, but it wasn't the "horrible" experience I was forecasting on either side.

This was the beginning of breaking down a barrier I had. Had I stuck to my same news sources, I would have maintained that barrier. I must admit if you are well entrenched on one side, you might have to dig deeper to remove the barrier and start bridging the divide.

Often, when we think of "the other side," we anticipate intense disagreements and fewer common beliefs, which leads us to avoid engaging in discourse. But we often misjudge our predicted emotional responses to disagreements; studies have shown that we often anticipate opposing views to be more disconcerting than they turn out to be, fueling our tendency for selective exposure.[10] So, just like watching a horror movie, reminding ourselves that the experience won't be as terrifying as we expect can help us keep an open mind (unless it's the movie where the girl's head swivels 360 degrees . . . that's definitely scary).

Finally, consider this. We generally avoid squabbles because we prefer a pat on the back over a slap on the wrist. We're likely to be more tolerant toward those we perceive as "our kind," but this can cause us to miss out on rich, enlightening conversations. Remember, embracing difference is the key to fostering meaningful discourse and understanding.

FROM DEEP CONVICTIONS TO COFFEE PREFERENCES

Think about this for a moment: Do you love pineapple on pizza? Or does the thought of it make you cringe? This preference might seem small, but it is, in fact, a belief—a low-commitment one. Now, imagine discussing climate change or the right to free speech—these are issues you're likely more invested in, and thus high-commitment beliefs.

When our high-commitment beliefs are challenged, it can feel like a personal attack, causing us to dig in our heels. The stakes feel higher because it's not just about "being right" but also about maintaining our understanding of the world and our place in it. A study I came across describes it perfectly: "Personal commitment to an attitude, belief, or behavior is presumed to increase defense motivation because of the greater discomfort produced by holding an incorrect view on an important issue."[11]

To illustrate this, let's look at Ava. Ava is deeply passionate about the environment and fervently believes in the urgency of tackling climate change. When she once met someone who denied climate change, she reacted vehemently, bordering on disrespect. Yet, when I teased her about her coffee brand choice, she merely laughed and shrugged it off. The difference? Her level of commitment to the two beliefs.

As you navigate your day-to-day conversations, it's helpful to keep this spectrum in mind. When you find yourself reacting strongly to a differing view, take a step back and ask, "Is this a high-commitment belief for me?" Recognizing this can help manage your reaction, reminding you that it's okay to disagree respectfully.

Also, remember that this goes both ways. When someone else reacts passionately during a conversation, it might be a sign that you've hit upon a high-commitment belief for them. Rather than pushing back, consider stepping into their shoes for a moment. This can open the doors to understanding, even in the face of disagreement.

In the end, it's not about who wins or loses the argument. It's about having open, respectful conversations where we can learn from each other. Just because someone disagrees with us, even on a deeply held belief, doesn't mean we should close the door on them. After all, isn't the world a more interesting place because of our different beliefs and perspectives?

DEHUMANIZING VERSUS HUMANIZING

Let's visit a gripping scene from the 1996 movie *A Time to Kill* and draw it closer to our hearts.

Imagine you're in a courtroom, the atmosphere thick with anticipation. The past days (or has it been weeks?) have been a whirlwind of emotions, arguments, and testimonies. At the center of it all is Carl Lee Hailey (portrayed brilliantly by Samuel L. Jackson), a father who, pushed to his limits, took the law into his hands to exact revenge on the men who had violated his precious little girl.

In steps Jake Brigance, a determined young lawyer (played by Matthew McConaughey). He knows he's fighting an uphill battle defending Carl Lee, a Black man in Mississippi who stands accused of killing two white men, however monstrous their crime might have been.

Now picture Jake, standing before the all-white jury in the courtroom, ready to make his closing argument. He looks each juror in the eye and asks them to close their eyes. His voice fills the room as he starts to paint a picture—an excruciatingly vivid image of a horrific crime committed against a defenseless ten-year-old girl.

He spares no detail, ensuring each member of the all-white jury can't escape the horrifying reality of what Carl Lee's daughter endured. It's a moment of gut-wrenching truth, as he brings everyone present face-to-face with the stark brutality of the assault and how she had been callously left to die. Then, the room falls deathly silent as Jake, fighting back tears, delivers his final, powerful line: "Can you see her? I want you to picture that little girl. *Now imagine she's white.*"

In that moment, Jake isn't just a lawyer seeking a favorable verdict. He's a voice challenging prejudice, questioning unconscious biases, and nudging each person in that room to step into another's shoes. He's hoping, praying, that the empathy this thought experiment might kindle will allow the jury to see past their racial prejudice and appreciate the desperation that led Carl Lee to his actions. He is challenging their perspective and how they choose to see this little girl.

This scene speaks to ways we may humanize some and dehumanize others based on a myriad of factors, including societal statutes, religion, ability, country of origin, race, tribe or caste, language, and gender, among others. While this movie is a work of fiction (as is the book on which it's based), the point is clear: we all humanize and dehumanize people in small and big ways. You may be wondering what it really means to dehumanize someone. To be clear, humanizing and dehumanizing is a spectrum and not strictly binary options. Let's explore this more.

Dehumanization: The Failure of Recognizing Shared Humanity

Dehumanization is defined as "the act of regarding, representing, or treating a person or group as less than human" and "the process of depriving a person or population of human qualities or attributes such as compassion, dignity, individuality, etc."[12] Dehumanization has also been described as a failure to see another as important as oneself. A dehumanized perspective regards other humans like animals or objects rather than fully developed human beings.[13] It often involves seeing others as illogical, unintelligent, irrational, and unsophisticated. A sense of superiority often fuels such perceptions, causing one to view oneself as the "superior self" in the interaction.

Dehumanization has been studied extensively in varying contexts. For instance, research has shown that women are dehumanized when sexualized or thought of as less competent. In one study, participants focusing on women's appearance rather than their personhood viewed them as lacking human nature, warmth, morality, and competence.[14] This pattern of dehumanization also extends to individuals of lower social status or those who provoke feelings of disgust.

Interestingly, the same study also highlighted that individuals who feel more socially connected (part of the in-crowd) were more likely to dehumanize others. This counterintuitive finding underscores the complex nature of dehumanization.[15] When you're in the in-crowd, it's easier to see outsiders as inferior (for example, how I view Android users as an Apple person . . . haha!). I've seen this happen in small and big ways. If you have ever been to a sporting event and seen someone wearing the opposing team's jersey in the home team's section, you probably know what I mean. While I've seen some light-hearted banter ensue, I've also seen major fistfights develop as a result.

Other factors also impact the increased potential of dehumanization. Personality characteristics have been explored in several studies. Hodson and Costello found that Canadians who scored higher on interpersonal disgust-proneness, the tendency to experience disgust in response to contact with strangers, were more likely to dehumanize immigrants.[16] More narcissistic individuals were especially likely to see others as less human than themselves.[17] And higher levels of psychopathy and autism were associated with the ascription of "less mind" to human targets.[18] Although these traits—emotional aversion, perceived superiority of the self, and callousness and social disconnection, respectively—are somewhat dissimilar, they all bear directly on interpersonal relations, and narcissism and psychopathy correlate moderately as elements of personality's "dark triad," alongside Machiavellianism. Tendencies to dehumanize others may be stronger among people who are disagreeable (callous and self-seeking), who experience strong emotional aversion to members of out-groups (perhaps especially in the context of xenophobic perceptions of immigrants), or who have diminished capacity for empathy or mentalizing.

Furthermore, power dynamics play a significant role in dehumanization. People in positions of power are more likely to dehumanize others, suggesting that awareness and conscious action are crucial in these scenarios. When one believes their title or position makes them better or gives them the ability to treat people however they want, it can create conditions ripe for dehumanization. Dehumanization also leads to less desire to help those in need, a lack of forgiveness, and generally less empathy toward others.[19] This impacts disagreements because we are less likely to try to understand someone we have dehumanized.

Humanization: The Act of Recognizing Shared Humanity

In contrast to dehumanization, *humanization* is the act of seeing others as equals, making someone or something seem gentler, kinder, or more appealing to people.[20] It involves recognizing their inherent worth, value, and dignity rather than creating it in one's mind. We see others as people (transformational) rather than as objects (transactional). This approach promotes genuine appreciation of others sharing their experiences with us. When we humanize others, it is easier to want to hear their story.

In the act of humanization, we choose to see others not as adversaries to be conquered but as individuals deserving of consideration. When we approach others from an equal standpoint—thinking *I can learn from anyone*—we shift from a *Superior Self* to an *Equal Self* perspective (more on this in a moment). This perspective requires intentionality and active efforts to understand and value others, even when their actions or choices may be disagreeable to us. You may be wondering how you can learn from or humanize abusive, manipulative, or controlling people. Humanizing in no way means staying in harmful relationships and/or continuing to be abused or harmed. There have been many relationships I have graciously severed not out of spite, but out of respect for myself (and for them).

Research has shown that increasing contact, sharing personal experiences with others, and focusing on similarities can help mitigate dehumanization.[21] This approach doesn't imply that you should avoid disagreements or polarized perspectives; instead, it calls for maintaining respect and humanization, even in the face of differing views or behaviors.

Dehumanization and Humanization in Society

The impacts of dehumanization are far-reaching, with macro examples from history, such as the treatment of Jewish people during the Holocaust, the perpetration of slavery, and societal attitudes toward people with disabilities. Political dehumanization continues to be an issue in countries all around the world, repeating the vicious cycle of dehumanizing a perceived "other."[22] In contrast, humanization can foster understanding, respect, and shared empathy among diverse groups of people. When exhibited by leaders in organizations and communities, it serves as an aspirational model for how to treat others. The process of shifting from dehumanization to humanization (summarized in table 5-1) is not binary, nor is it a neat or easy task; in fact, it's a complex and often messy endeavor. Yet it is vitally important and achievable with conscious effort. It's a task each one of us must undertake to foster empathy, compassion, and understanding in society. As you navigate this journey, it's crucial to remember these words: *I may disagree with their views and choices, but I still can choose to agree with their humanity.*

One small but major way to move through the spectrum of dehumanizing to humanizing is by changing how we see both ourselves and our ideological other. When we are able to positively reframe, we can navigate disagreements in a more empathetic way.

TABLE 5-1: Dehumanization vs. Humanization

DEHUMANIZATION	HUMANIZATION
Sees others as less competent or intelligent	Recognizes others' competence and intellect
Views others as objects	Views others as people
Views others as adversaries	Displays compassion toward others
Is rooted in a Superior Self perspective	Is rooted in an Equal Self perspective
Leads to social exclusion and lack of empathy	Encourages inclusivity and empathy
Is common in high-power positions and requires little effort	Requires intentional consistent action in positions of power

THE 3SELF MODEL

Our perception of self is a critical factor in our interactions with others. This section explores the three distinct yet inter-connected aspects of self-perception—the Inferior Self, the Superior Self, and the Equal Self—that compose a framework my team and I created called the 3Self Model. This model can help you better understand your attitudes, biases, and responses in various contexts.

Inferior Self

To start our discussion of the Inferior Self, let's look at the American Psychological Association's definition of *inferiority complex*: a "basic feeling of inadequacy and insecurity, deriving from actual or imagined physical or psychological deficiency."[23] This description aligns with the concept of the Inferior Self, where one devalues oneself and harbors feelings of inadequacy, leading to self-sabotaging behaviors or accepting mistreatment from others.

While I am not completely free of operating in the Inferior Self, I spent a lot of my time growing up here. Because of the abuse, constant bullying, and lack of resources in my life, I always wondered what was wrong with me. I wondered why I didn't have both parents in my life consistently. I blamed myself for all the ills that I encountered, and I approached many situations from a "less-than" perspective. This led me either to be passive aggressive and disrespect-fully agree because I desired acceptance, or to disrespect-fully disagree because I was trying to prove to myself and others that I was "good enough." What about you? When you operate from the Inferior Self, how does that show up in your conversations and disagreements? Do you also feel like you have to prove something or, on the opposite end of the spectrum, do you shrink from being assertive and sharing your truth?

A manifestation of this inferiority is what I call "inferiorcentrism," a focus on why we perceive ourselves as "not enough" compared to others we think are innately better. When we have disagreements with them, we feel that they obviously are better and so we suppress what we really think or feel. We look up to them, and we look down on ourselves.

You can manage this unhealthy mindset by doing the following:

- Recall instances where your thoughts or actions positively impacted others.

- Acknowledge that growth and learning are continuous journeys that we are all undertaking.

- Seek professional counseling to gain tools and insights to manage your feelings of inferiority.

Superior Self

At the other end of the spectrum is the Superior Self, an inflated sense of self-worth that often leads to the dehumanization and disrespect of others. The ego takes center stage, devaluing others in an attempt to uphold its superiority. An example from my personal life involves a trip to Frankie's, one of my kids' favorite entertainment parks in Charlotte, North Carolina. The last time my daughter had been there, she'd noticed a sign saying they weren't admitting anyone under eighteen after 3 p.m. While we were on our way there, she tried to tell me we wouldn't be able to enter, but I talked over her and told her there was no way that would happen. I *listened* to my daughter, but I did not *hear* her.

I was convinced that what she told me didn't make sense; based on my experience, places enforced that rule only when the kids weren't with an adult. Instead of listening to my daughter and calling ahead, I operated from my Superior Self (because obviously I knew more than she did . . . ha!). We arrived at Frankie's at 3:30 p.m. and I saw the sign and tried to walk in with my kids. I was promptly stopped and told that no one younger than eighteen could enter. I retorted (now trying to defend my error) that I was their dad and I would be responsible for them. They acknowledged my statement but told me that was their rule. I walked back to the car like a dog with its tail between its legs, frustrated by this asinine policy. I turned to my daughter, apologized for not really hearing her, and then offered to take us bowling somewhere else.

Why is this important to know? The Superior Self can easily creep up in our everyday life. You might be thinking, *Justin, you were just being a parent*, but even as parents we can disrespectfully disagree with our kids, and this was one of many examples in my life. Yes, I am charged to lead my kids well, but that doesn't mean I can't hear and honor their perspectives too. If I operated from my Equal Self, I would have picked up the phone and called ahead. There is hope for us as we become more aware of what we're thinking and feeling in our interactions not only with our kids but also with our ideological others.

To navigate away from this superiority, you can:

◘ Confront your biases to promote personal growth. For instance, consider the discussion in my book *The Inclusive Mindset* about Black women in relationships with white men. Stay open-minded before forming a judgment.[24]

◘ Cultivate an openness to alternative perspectives. Try to understand how someone else could be right in their viewpoint.

◻ Listen to diverse stories that provide alternative view-points, either online or in person.

◻ Request feedback on your beliefs and positions to gain a more balanced perspective.

Equal Self

The Equal Self, which represents an ideal state of balance, recognizes the inherent worth of oneself and others. It's about seeing everyone as equals, valuing their rights, feelings, and experiences.

A person operating from their Equal Self is both compassionate and full of conviction. They can hold to the truth that what they feel is valuable and important, while also holding space for others and new information and perspectives. When operating from the Equal Self, you don't need to prove yourself; you are simply being yourself.

———

As we interact with others, we often oscillate between these three states, influenced by our environment, power dynamics, and the individuals we encounter. The key to maintaining balance is awareness and consistent effort. Ask yourself what self you might be operating from in this moment and what you can do to move to Equal Self.

To be clear, we will never operate 100 percent of the time in Equal Self. We all have moments of weakness and are impacted by our fears, feelings, and focus. The goal here isn't perfection but awareness and progression. The more aware we are, the better we can navigate new paths of learning as we challenge our perspectives.

Remember, shifting from Superior Self and Inferior Self toward Equal Self requires conscious effort, self-awareness, and a willingness to continually learn and grow. Each interaction is an opportunity to engage the 3Self Model, improving ourselves and our relationships with others as we strive to spend more time operating in Equal Self and learn to respectfully disagree more.

THE DANCE OF CONVERSATIONAL RECEPTIVENESS

Let's imagine conversations as a dance. Think of the last time you danced (okay, maybe not that one time). *Conversational receptiveness* is the rhythm that holds it all together. It's not about winning the dance-off, but about appreciating the music that your partner is dancing to. It means being curious about why they move the way they do, even if their style is different from yours.

Of course, being open to new dance styles doesn't mean we should accept them all unconditionally. But not every dance style different from ours should be dismissed immediately. Being receptive means giving people the chance to show us their steps, even if at first they seem strange or unfamiliar.

Those with a knack for the dance of conversation don't rush to judge new moves. They're patient, taking the time to understand why someone dances the way they do. It's not about copying every move, but about appreciating the thought and experience that formed it.

However, there can be stumbling blocks on the dance floor of conversation. As we previously discussed, one is naïve realism—the belief that we're dancing to the one and only "right" rhythm, while everyone else is offbeat. This reminds me of a time I attended a silent disco. Everyone wore headphones and could switch among three DJs, who were all playing different music. It was very interesting to watch: people appeared to be dancing offbeat but in reality were listening to different music altogether. Another stumbling block on the dance floor of conversation is "negative newness"—when we think someone's dance style is more alien than it really is, simply because we've never seen it before.

To overcome these barriers, we need to remind ourselves that trying a new dance might not be as scary as we think, and that some people might actually be listening to different music. We can better understand their "dancing" by listening to their music—which doesn't mean that we must like it, or even choose to listen to it again. By managing our expectations, we become more open-minded. We're not just sticking to our own rhythm but taking a step toward understanding someone else's.

Finally, conversational receptiveness isn't just about the moves, but also about the words we say as we dance. It's about showing through our language that we're genuinely interested in others' rhythm. In addition to the words themselves, it's about the spirit behind them—a spirit of understanding and respect for different dance styles. The ultimate goal is to create a dance floor where differences in style don't lead to battles but instead to richer, more inclusive choreography.

While I know you're excited about going out and dancing for real now, first I want you to see how you can apply these skill sets in everyday experiences like dancing (you don't dance every day?) and having disagreements. Instead of immediately dismissing a dance move, you can choose to learn the move itself or what inspired the person to dance that way in order to challenge your perspective and move closer to respectful disagreements.

PILLAR 1 RECAP:
CHALLENGE YOUR PERSPECTIVE

To challenge your perspectives, you must actively seek out alternative viewpoints and question your own assumptions. Here are some actions you can take to implement this pillar:

◘ **Seek diverse perspectives.** Surround yourself with individuals from different backgrounds, cultures, and beliefs. Actively engage in discussions and events that challenge your worldview and expose you to new ideas. Choose to see the value of every human being regardless of stance, status, and background.

◘ **Read broadly.** Explore literature, articles, and books from various genres, authors, and perspectives. Delve into subjects you are unfamiliar with to broaden your knowledge and understanding.

REFLECTIONS AND ACTIONS

1. In disagreements, which of the three selves (Superior, Equal, or Inferior) do you tend to operate from and why?

2. What is one way that you tend to dehumanize others in a disagreement (e.g., talking over someone and not listening), and what is one way you can begin progressing toward better humanizing them?

3. When have you found it hard to humanize others you disagree with and why? What is one thing you can do to better humanize them?

CHAPTER 6

The Teacher Appears When the Student Is Ready

Pillar 2, Be the Student

This chapter focuses on the importance of placing yourself in a position to constantly learn and provides insights on how to do so in practice. Use this chapter to develop more of a learner's mindset as you meet people and experience those you disagree with.

In the quiet suburbia of Dayton, Ohio, a couple named Robert and Michelle lived a harmonious life—or so it seemed. Robert, a professor of political science at the local university, was a gifted orator with a knack for argumentation. Michelle, a brilliant economist running her own consulting firm, was well versed in the intricacies of financial markets and policies.

At social gatherings and parties, the couple was the epicenter of intellectual conversations, with Robert often using his academic prowess to hold the room captive, while Michelle would enthrall people with her insightful economic analyses. However, at home, things were quite different.

Over time, a pattern had emerged. Whenever the couple found themselves in a disagreement, whether it was about who left the dishes unwashed or whose turn it was to walk the dog, Robert always seemed to take over the conversation. His professorial instincts would kick in, and he would launch into a lecture of sorts, drawing from political theories and historical precedents to validate his points. While Michelle was equipped to argue her point from an economic perspective, it seemed like Robert was always more interested in lecturing rather than listening.

The most striking disagreement happened when they were planning a major investment in a new house. Michelle, with her economic background, had analyzed the market trends and real estate data and was convinced that it was the right time to make an investment. Robert, however, saw this decision from a political standpoint. He argued about political stability, potential policy changes, and economic uncertainties, citing multiple historical events.

In this heated discussion, Robert was so consumed in proving his point and lecturing about political implications that he hardly paid any attention to Michelle's economic analysis. Whenever she tried to share her perspective, he would immediately jump in about why her point wasn't valid. Robert would alternate between sitting and standing as they argued, standing only when he disagreed with her point in a subconscious effort to dominate the conversation and prove his point. The discussion turned into a one-sided debate, leaving Michelle feeling unheard and frustrated.

One day, unable to bear this pattern any longer, Michelle confronted Robert. "Our disagreements," she said, "should be opportunities for us to understand each other's perspectives, not platforms for you to lecture. I value your knowledge, but I need you to value mine as well."

Robert was taken aback. He had failed to realize that his penchant for debate had been suffocating their discussions. He realized that while he had been focusing on teaching Michelle about his perspective, he had forgotten to learn from her economic wisdom.

Robert chose to share this moment with his therapist to gain better clarity and insight. He was able to see his pattern of lecturing and not really listening to Michelle. Robert resolved to make a conscious effort to listen more and lecture less during their disagreements. When he caught himself cutting Michelle off in conversations, he would stop and apologize to her for doing it. He tried to summarize the point she just made back to her before he shared any new points of his own. These small changes began to help Robert appreciate Michelle's point of view and acknowledge her expertise. On the other hand, Michelle found a newfound respect for Robert's ability to change and adapt. Their disagreements, instead of being draining, became constructive, making their relationship even stronger. They learned not just to argue but to listen, understand, and grow together.

Robert chose to lean into the learner's mindset, where he recognized opportunities to learn from not only Michelle but his colleagues as well. Why is this important? Some of us have grown so accustomed to social media "conversations," which in reality are often monologues where posters simply share what they believe the world should know, without any discussion. One step toward having a genuine conversation is to embrace a learner's mindset.

THE LEARNER'S MINDSET

As defined on the 360Learning blog, "a learner's mindset is when an individual considers every new experience as an opportunity to learn. People who possess this mentality can adapt to their surroundings better and absorb information faster."[1] This reminds me of something my mother would instill in my brother and me: "Always be a learner!" She challenged us to learn from anyone, whether the unhoused person under the bridge, the custodial staff at the college where she worked, or the dean of a department. She taught us that we could learn from anyone at any time if we chose to. She empowered us to always be a student!

Have you ever heard that "the teacher appears when the student is ready"? This statement implies that we can really learn only when we're open and willing to listen. Have you ever tried to share something new with someone who did not appear interested in listening to what you had to say? Now reverse it: Have you ever done that to someone who was trying to teach you something new? I believe most of us have done it; I certainly have. If we really want to have respectful disagreements, then we need to do a better job of choosing to listen and not lecturing, where it is only your point that matters and there's no dialogue.

My Kenya Trip

In 2003, as a young, ambitious twenty-something, I found myself touching down on the rich, red soil of Kenya for the first time. It was a journey I'd embarked on with a sense of exhilaration, mixed with a dash of youthful arrogance. I was there to serve the leader of our organization, a seasoned veteran, and his colleagues, who bore the wisdom of ages; they had experienced more than twice as much life as I had. (Note: I am not calling them old.)

My heart pounded with the urge to prove myself, to mark my existence in that space, to let them know that I, too, was someone to reckon with—not just a young fledgling but a repository of knowledge. Yet, in this relentless pursuit to demonstrate my worth, I lost sight of something profoundly significant: the opportunity to learn.

It was my mentor, Carlos, a figure of quiet wisdom, who saw my struggle. He saw me trying to jump into conversations. He saw me impose myself by sitting in the middle of the group and immediately piping up to share my perspective. He saw me trying to prove my worth rather than simply *being* my worth.

One warm afternoon, in a corner of our conference room, he gently nudged me as he saw me trying to lecture this group about my perspective. He asked me to be a fly on the wall, to observe, to listen, and to absorb. He challenged me, explaining that it wasn't my job to reshape the world with my fresh but limited wisdom; instead, I was there to serve, to learn from the experiences and insights of those who had walked the paths I was only beginning to tread.

The realization was a heavy one, but it set me free. I discovered that I had been so consumed in teaching, in giving unsolicited lectures, that I had forgotten to learn. The dynamics of power and knowledge seemed complicated, but the solution was surprisingly simple—I needed to become a student again, to tap into the humility of learning.

I call it the "fly-on-the-wall principle." It doesn't mean I have to remain silent or invisible all the time, but it encourages me to be a sponge, soaking up knowledge from those around me. This principle, born from the heart of Kenya, has since traveled with me to countless boardrooms and coffee shops, steering my interactions with peers and team members.

Being a student has never diminished my worth; instead, it has enriched it. It has allowed me to learn, to grow, and to build an arsenal of wisdom that I can now share more meaningfully. I find that the lessons I've learned in the silence of observation are the ones that resonate the most when I do serve the role of a teacher. The paradox of it all is that, by embracing the role of a student, I've become a better—more insightful, more empathetic—teacher.

My journey from the city streets of Kenya to where I am now is a testament to the fact that sometimes our greatest strength lies in listening, in learning. The journey to wisdom does not always begin with a lecture but often with a silent pledge to remain a perpetual student, open to the world and its endless lessons.

I tell you this story to encourage you to heed the wisdom of Carlos and choose to be a learner. The question that lies ahead is whether we will choose to learn when faced with both the internal and external barriers of learning.

The Inverted U

The inverted U concept, or the Yerkes-Dodson law, states that our performance (or learning) is at an optimal state when we are slightly excited but not stressed out.[2] This law can also apply to our perceived knowledge and its impact on learning. You can think of this as a continuum with "knowing nothing" at one end, "knowing everything" at the other, and an optimal learning zone somewhere in the middle.

At the "knowing nothing" extreme, a person may feel overwhelmed or unsure where to start, which can hinder motivation and engagement. It could lead to feelings of inadequacy or even evoke fear of failure, which can impede the learning process.

At the "knowing everything" end of the spectrum, a person may become complacent or overly confident. This can prevent them from seeking new information, questioning their understanding, or staying open to alternative perspectives.

As a result, learning stagnates because there's no perceived need for further knowledge or skill acquisition.

The peak of the inverted U represents an optimal state of perceived knowledge. In this state, an individual acknowledges that they know something but also understands that there's more to learn. They are confident enough to engage with the material, yet humble enough to recognize their limitations. This balanced mindset promotes curiosity, fosters resilience, and encourages an ongoing commitment to learning.

In summary, the inverted U concept in learning, in relation to perceived knowledge, suggests an optimal point where a balance between knowing and not knowing fosters the best learning outcomes. Both underconfidence and overconfidence can negatively impact learning, emphasizing the need for a balanced, growth-oriented mindset. This is one reason why, in the Work. Meaningful. learning experiences, my colleagues and I encourage participants to remember a time when they learned something new or that was challenging. Realizing they've done it before helps build their confidence. My team and I also encourage participants to think of moments in their life when they were proven wrong (which, of course, has never happened to me). The participants often share that their new learning or way of thinking was inspired by someone else.

LEARNING FROM OTHERS

Just think about it: when we are learning-minded, we can learn so much from each other. As an ancient proverb wisely reminds us, "Intelligent people are always ready to learn. Their ears are open for knowledge."[3] That's a pretty cool way to think about intelligence, right? It's not about how many facts we can recite, but how much we're willing to learn from others.

And you know what? Learning from others doesn't mean we always have to agree with them. It's about showing them respect. Say you're grabbing coffee with a friend, and they share their opinion about something. You might not see eye to eye, but you listen and try to understand where they're coming from. That's what it's all about.

In fact, every conversation we have is an opportunity to learn. I've picked up as many life lessons from people who've made mistakes as I have from those who seem to have it all figured out, and those in between. It's like getting two-for-one lessons: learning what to do, and what not to do. Think about your own experiences. Haven't you learned a lot from both great and not-so-great bosses?

Sometimes we forget that everyone loves to express their opinion. Research has found that "people systematically underestimate the affective benefits others derive from expressing their opposing opinions."[4] Simply put, we all want to be heard, and sometimes we forget to listen. That's when misunderstandings and conflicts can happen. Remember this when you're deep in conversation: be open to the other person, and learn from each other. If both parties are just talking to be heard and not listening, there really is no conversation.

Now, let's stroll down memory lane. You might remember believing in Santa Claus as a kid. And then, one day, you heard from a friend at school that Santa isn't real (that kid should have been given extra nap time). You might have defended your belief tooth and nail, but eventually, you accepted the new reality. There have probably been many other beliefs you've adjusted or abandoned as you've grown, right?

Or think about how wary we used to be about having a new teacher at school. We felt they had something to prove and were a bit strict. But over time, we realized they were just trying to establish their style of teaching. It's a lot like when we learn something new. Initially, we might be overly enthusiastic about it, but with time, we gain a deeper understanding of how to share it with others.

As my wise friend Hassan Ghiassi once told me, "The answer you seek may be one conversation away." Isn't that something? We're not meant to go through life alone, figuring everything out by ourselves. We're meant to connect, share experiences, and learn from each other. It's like we're all stars in a huge, vast constellation of human beings. So, let's open up, get ready to listen, and learn from each other. After all, that's what makes life such an exciting journey.

LEARNING TO LISTEN, LISTENING TO LEARN

Imagine that you're mid-conversation, not as the main speaker but as a keen learner. A nugget of wisdom from *The Anatomy of Peace* resonates here: "It is no good trying to teach if I myself am not listening and learning."[5] Isn't that a perspective changer? This insight beautifully frames the essence of true conversation—not merely to respond but to listen, learn, and grow.

Here's a little surprise: listening can also turn you into a persuasion pro. According to a *Harvard Business Review* article, "When we appear receptive to listening to and respecting others' opposing positions, they find our arguments to be more persuasive." It means listening doesn't just make conversations more engaging, but it makes you—yes, you—more convincing.[6]

To be clear, this isn't about using tricks and techniques to get the other person to adopt your view, but rather it's an unintended benefit of genuinely listening to others.

Now, let's transport you into a passionate discussion. Freeze. Ask yourself, *What if they're right?* How would that question rewire the course of the conversation? Would it affect your approach, perhaps soften your words? Challenging ourselves to consider this perspective can lead to profound, meaningful exchanges.

Now, hold up a mirror to your conversational style. Do you tend to dismiss or seek connection? Do you listen only to refute or to truly understand? James Robilotta, a dear friend and authenticity expert, posed this fascinating question to me one day: "What if we listened like we are actually wrong?"

In my book *The Inclusive Mindset*, I discuss an approach called the Power of 3, which breaks down listening into levels.[7] Level 1 is where we hear the words and are ready to throw our two cents in. Level 2 is when we've asked a question, and the speaker has responded twice. But the real magic happens at Level 3, where we've allowed the speaker to share their viewpoint at least three times before we join in with our thoughts. It's like giving them the stage to fully express their feelings and perspectives.

Imagine chatting with a friend who excitedly tells you about a fantastic new seafood restaurant they've just tried. Instead of diving deeper into their experience, you instinctively cut in, "But have you tried this other place?" Unintentionally, we've just stolen the conversation's spotlight. We've failed to reach Level 3 listening, where we fully engage to understand their words, their excitement, the flavors they tasted—the whole nine yards. What if we did this even when we disagreed with someone? How much more would we understand their perspective?

It can be tough to dive deeper into a perspective that you find unsavory. If you ever find yourself stuck in a conversation, grasping at straws about what to say next, try this golden phrase: "Tell me more." This simple invitation can spark the speaker to reveal more, leading to a richer dialogue. In fact, a study in the *Journal of Experimental Psychology* found that expressed interest significantly influences conversation's flow and outcome.[8]

Also, it's okay to admit when you're out of your depth. Saying something like, "I don't know much about X, but I'm eager to learn," can foster open, authentic conversations. Haven't we all been in that awkward situation of pretending to be a know-it-all? A little humility can take off that pressure and open up space for genuine learning. Nod your head three times if you've ever acted like you know something you didn't (now stop before your book club members know what section you're in).

Lastly, let's ponder why we sometimes dive headlong into arguments. Often, we're not out to solve a problem; we're there for a feel-good rush. When disagreements spiral into disrespect, it's often because we find a guilty pleasure in rebutting the other person's viewpoint. By recognizing this, we can curb our knee-jerk reactions and create healthier, more constructive discussions.

Mastering the art of listening to learn and learning to listen is a journey that takes time and practice. But oh, it's a journey worth embarking upon! Every conversation becomes a window into another person's world, a stepping-stone to growth, and a bridge to connection. Let's dive into this adventure with an open heart and a willing mind.

COMPREHENSION: SEEKING TO UNDERSTAND

I love the ancient proverb that says, "Fools have no interest in understanding; they only want to air their own opinions."

Ever felt like you're in a school play, where everyone expects you to remember your lines, nail your timing, and never miss a beat? You might have even thought that's what learning is all about—getting everything right in one shot. But that's like trying to drink a smoothie in one gulp without tasting the berries or feeling the cool swirl on your tongue. Learning is more about comprehending, or in smoothie terms, savoring the blend. This is the essence of Pillar 2: Be the Student. It's about absorbing the flavors, digesting the ingredients, and letting the nutrients work their magic.

This idea extends into our conversations, especially when we're talking with folks who see things differently. It's like we're trying a new recipe, and instead of tasting it, we just read the instructions back to the chef. Sure, rephrasing what they said can make it seem like we're listening, but it's more important to taste the words, to comprehend what they're saying. And let's be clear—we're not doing this to convince them that our recipe is better. It's about valuing their unique mix of ingredients, acknowledging the care they put into their preparation, and savoring the diversity of flavors in the world of ideas.

But remember, understanding isn't an instant thing. Sometimes, you need to taste something several times before you can appreciate all its nuances. I imagine a wise food critic saying, "Receptiveness to new flavors necessitates sampling them over time." It's about patience, persistence, and being open to the surprise of a delayed "yum!" The idea of having continued conversations—not a simple one-and-done taste—is helpful here.

Why make such a big deal about comprehension in conversation? The pursuit of comprehension is not merely an optional enhancement to conversation; it's a necessity because it:

- **Deepens understanding.** Comprehension is the key to unlocking the layers of thought, emotion, and ideas within a conversation. It's about grasping the full picture, the totality of the message being communicated.

□ **Promotes empathy.** Comprehension also allows us to step into the other's shoes more effectively, to feel their emotions and understand their perspective.

□ **Prevents miscommunication.** Comprehension minimizes the potential for misunderstanding. It's not just about hearing words; it's about fully absorbing the speaker's intent.

□ **Strengthens relationships.** By demonstrating a commitment to understanding, we signal to the speaker that their viewpoint matters to us. This fosters trust, respect, and connection.

□ **Enhances learning.** The pursuit of comprehension is a direct route to learning. It opens our minds to new perspectives, ideas, and experiences, enriching our personal and professional lives.

□ **Facilitates problem-solving.** Comprehension is also a precursor to effective problem-solving. It helps to identify root causes and paves the way for more effective solutions.

In essence, seeking comprehension transforms listening from a passive act into an active process that nurtures connection, growth, and understanding. It shifts our mindset from just hearing the words to truly understanding the message (yes, even when we disagree).

Interestingly, research suggests that we pay more attention to strangers in conversation because we are learning about them, whereas with people we know, we tend to fill in the blanks based on our existing knowledge.[9] This assumption can be a hindrance when people we know introduce new information or perspectives. In the next chapter, we'll discuss the importance of filling these blanks with curiosity, not conclusions. We'll explore how to keep our understanding fresh and dynamic, which enables us to engage more deeply and effectively with everyone we interact with, irrespective of our level of familiarity with them.

PILLAR 2 RECAP: BE THE STUDENT

"Be the student" means adopting a mindset of constant learning and personal growth. Here are some strategies to help you embody this pillar:

- **Set learning goals.** Identify specific areas of interest or skills you would like to develop. Set achievable goals and create a plan to acquire new knowledge or enhance your existing abilities.

- **Seek feedback.** Actively seek feedback from mentors, peers, or experts in the field you wish to grow in. Be open to constructive criticism and use it as an opportunity for improvement.

- **Reflect on experiences.** Take time to reflect on your experiences and identify lessons learned. Analyze both your successes and failures to extract valuable insights that will contribute to your personal and professional development.

REFLECTIONS AND ACTIONS

1. Think of a recent time when you learned something new (how to ski, a new language, a mindfulness practice, etc.). What did you learn about and what did you learn about yourself as you learned it?

2. In a future disagreement, practice the Power of 3, where you listen to Level 3 of the conversation. Focus on seeking comprehension of a different perspective.

3. In a conversation today or tomorrow, use the phrase "tell me more" to keep the conversation going and focused on understanding what that person said.

CHAPTER 7

Don't Take the Exit on People

Pillar 3, Cultivate Your Curiosity

T his chapter focuses on filling the gaps in our understanding with curiosity, not conclusions. Use this chapter to learn how to not take the "exit" of assumptions with others, but instead continue to be curious.

In the fall of 2018, I found myself grappling with a deep-seated anger. I couldn't shake off thoughts about my dad's absence throughout my childhood. My parents divorced when I was just four. Initially, I saw my dad every other weekend, but gradually, our meetings dwindled to once a month, then to years of silence. My dad lived in Detroit (2.5 hours from Grand Rapids), and the fact that I didn't see him often became my new normal. The challenging relationship between my parents didn't make things any easier. At the time, I found solace in simple things like skating and hanging out with friends.

I want to clarify that I understand that many people endure challenging childhoods even with both parents around. However, as I matured, the emotional toll of my father's absence became harder for me to bear. During my early thirties, I often found myself breaking down, questioning what I had done to push my dad away. My pain was particularly intense on Father's Day, a holiday that frequently reduced me to tears. I often felt so overwhelmed that I couldn't even manage to reach out. My anger kept simmering beneath the surface.

In the summer of 2019, I planned a trip to Ghana, where my dad now resides, with my kids. It was their first visit, and I intended to use the opportunity to confront my dad. I wanted to ask him why he hadn't fought for me more, why he let our relationship suffer because of the issues between my mother and him. I was prepared to unload years of pent-up resentment.

However, a remarkable therapist and my supportive cohort from Leadership Charlotte encouraged me to adopt a different approach. Instead of confronting my dad, I was urged to go and hear his story.

So, I chose to ask him about his life and his feelings about our strained relationship. I voiced my hurt, not to blame him but to express my experiences honestly. Despite my dissatisfaction with the past, I was committed to improving our future relationship. I decided to view my dad as a human with his own complexities, and I was determined to maintain our connection. Even during my annual trips to Ghana, I choose to spend time with him. On a recent trip, my stepmother showed me a very old letter I had never seen, in which he communicated his love for me as a child.

These moments helped shift my mindset and allowed us to forge a better relationship, but I had to be open to having my perspective challenged. I had to approach him and the situation as a student ready to learn. I also had to lean into being more curious and asking questions, rather than jumping to (and sticking to) my conclusions.

My father and I might never agree on his past decisions, but I've learned that I can control my reactions and shape my future, and it all started by not taking the exit on my dad and our shared experiences.

WHAT IS THE EXIT?

Isn't it disconcerting when you find out someone has been talking about you, but not to you? There's a level of disconnect there, an unsettling sense of being observed without being engaged. And yet we often unwittingly do the same thing to others, especially those who exist outside our comfortable spheres of interaction. We neglect them, take the exit on them, often without even realizing we're doing so.

The key to fostering empathy and understanding among people is to not take the exit on them, but instead build bridges and open doors. We need to expand our circles of grace to invite them in.

Remember, our circles of grace are those cozy bubbles of comfort composed of family, friends, those we resonate with, and those that we hold dear. We lean on these circles for knowledge, support, and emotional growth. But when we encounter individuals who don't fit into these familiar spaces, we often find ourselves defaulting to taking the exit.

Our brains have a natural predisposition toward this behavior, toward focusing on familiar territory and avoiding what seems unfamiliar. It's a survival mechanism designed to conserve energy and optimize brain capacity.[1]

Consider this scenario: Every weekday you drive the same route to work, and on Saturdays, you take the same exit (maybe for a regular weekend ritual). But one Sunday, you're meant to continue straight instead of taking your regular exit. However, out of habit, you find yourself taking the exit anyway. This illustrates how we often interact with people outside our circles. Right before we get to know them, right before we learn more about their true self, we veer away—we take the exit and will be stuck in the traffic of knowledge gaps full of assumptions.

However, we can train ourselves to break this cycle. This requires intentionality—a conscious effort to stay on the path, to invest time in understanding these new individuals, to delve deeper into their lives and experiences. By doing this, we're not only building bridges of empathy, but also expanding our circles of grace. We engage those who may differ from us not by taking the exit, but by welcoming them into our journey, thereby enriching our lives and theirs.

Why We Take the Exit

Research conducted by Matthew Leonard's team at the University of California, San Francisco, has shown that the human brain can "fill in" inaudible parts of speech through a process called perceptual restoration. The team discovered that one region of the brain, the inferior frontal cortex, predicts what word a person is likely to hear even before the superior temporal gyrus, which contains the audio cortex, begins processing the sounds. To gather data, the study used epilepsy patients who had electrodes implanted in their brains for seizure monitoring.

Participants were played recordings of a word that could be either *faster* or *factor*, but with the middle sound replaced by noise. The data showed that the participants' brains responded as though they had heard the missing *s* or *c* sound, illustrating the brain's ability to overcome real-world interruptions. However, the study also found that the brain's predictive abilities have limitations. It doesn't seem to use the context of a conversation to enhance the accuracy of its pre-dictions. For instance, even when participants were primed with a certain context, they were just as likely to hear *factor* as they were to hear *faster*.[2]

Likewise, it's very possible that in disrespectful disagree-ments we don't take the time to make sure we are disagreeing about the same thing. A practical tip to dive deeper is to ask the other person what they mean by X or how they define X. This is one reason why I've clearly identified what I mean by respect, because I realized that often when people have challenged my premise of respectfully disagreeing, we were misaligned on how we defined respect.

Often we "take the exit" simply because our brains want to conserve energy, not because we just don't want to engage people or their perspectives (although this is sometimes the case). Our brains try to fill in the blanks and to turn the dotted lines into details for processing.

The Dotted Line Dilemma

Have you ever stumbled upon a sentence that stopped midway, hanging in suspense like a high-wire trapeze artist frozen in midair? An incomplete thought, trailing off, invites you not just to complete its narrative but to imbue it with your unique perceptions and experiences.

Imagine the following statement made by a faceless stranger on the internet: "Drivers who drive on the left side of the street are. . . ." Now freeze. What rushes to fill that void, that ellipsis? What are the words that bubble up from your subconscious to complete that sentence?

The way you fill that void highlights not just who you are but where you come from. In areas like the United States, Canada, Ghana, China, or parts of Latin America, you might instinctively complete that sentence with ". . . inviting disaster," reflecting the commonality of right-hand driving in these regions.

On the contrary, if you call India, Jamaica, South Africa, the UK, Australia, or New Zealand home, you might respond with ". . . simply navigating their daily commute." That's because in these nations, driving on the left is the norm.

How curious it is that the blanks we fill are reflections of our own worlds, colored by our cultural, geographical, and personal lenses! The very first response that ought to come to our mind upon hearing that incomplete sentence isn't an assumption about the person, but rather a simple question: Where is this person from or where have they traveled recently?

This example highlights the danger of assumption. When we fill in the blanks with our own understanding rather than facts, we inadvertently sketch a distorted image of the person we're trying to understand. This is what I call the Dotted Line Dilemma. By attempting to fill in the dotted lines without all the necessary information, we run the risk of misunderstanding and misjudging people, resulting in misguided interactions and relationships. *When we don't understand context, we draw our own conclusions, and that's the beginning of catastrophic communication.*

The Dotted Line Dilemma is deeply rooted in our discomfort with uttering the phrase "tell me more." I have found that discomfort lies in a cultural fallacy. In today's society, listening and being curious have been falsely equated to accepting someone's ideas. To not take the exit on people, we must challenge this falsehood. Saying "tell me more" helps us do this by not only reflecting our desire to learn, but also opening the door to a richer, more nuanced understanding of others. By resisting our instinct to fill in the blanks and seeking to know more, we allow space for authentic connections and deeper relationships. This represents a shift from conclusions to curiosity, promoting active learning rather than clinging to preconceived ideas.

The Illusion of Asymmetric Insight

Sometimes we are so engrossed in our own interpretations and assumptions that we fail to see the full picture. We rush to agree or disagree without fully understanding what we are agreeing or disagreeing with. We judge, label, and categorize people without truly knowing them. These behaviors stem from what psychologists call the *illusion of asymmetric insight*, the conviction that we know others better than they know us. This psychological bias is fueled by our ego, our desire to feel superior, and our need to fit everything neatly into our worldviews. It becomes problematic when it governs our interactions and relationships, as it stifles open-mindedness and genuine understanding.

The illusion of asymmetric insight is essentially when you feel that you're a bit of a mind reader but that others can't quite get you. Think about a situation with your best friend. You might think, *I know them so well, I can predict exactly how they're going to react,* while at the same time, *They couldn't possibly predict all my reactions; I have too many sides they haven't seen.*

Research suggests that individuals who resist the illusion of asymmetric insight are more successful in their personal and professional relationships. They are better listeners, more empathetic, and less likely to engage in conflicts resulting from misunderstandings.[3]

This belief extends beyond one-on-one relationships to whole groups. Imagine you're a cat person in a group of dog people. You might think, *I totally get why they love dogs—dogs are loyal, energetic, and playful. But they just don't understand why I love cats. They don't get the independent spirit of cats, the quiet companionship.*

We all are complex, and we all have the ability to understand each other deeply—it's about open communication, empathetic listening, and acknowledging that no one is as simple as they seem. The awareness that we might not know as much as we think we do can help us avoid falling victim to the Dotted Line Dilemma and the illusion of asymmetric insight, and represents a big step forward for courageous curiosity.

To summarize, the Dotted Line Dilemma poses a serious challenge to building effective and authentic relationships. The way to avoid it is by fostering a culture of curiosity, actively learning, and resisting the illusion of asymmetric insight. You must make a conscious effort to not "fill in the blanks" about others based on your assumptions, but instead to earnestly seek to understand them as they truly are.

WHY CURIOSITY MATTERS

If you have had the combination of a TV and kids (whether your own or ones you had watch over), you might have come across *Curious George*. Based on the book series of the same name, *Curious George* is a delightful animated TV show that captures the fun and excitement of exploring the world around us. The show is centered on George, a mischievous yet endearing little monkey, whose curiosity often gets him into unexpected situations—think of a toddler getting into cupboards or touching everything in a grocery store!

George lives with his friend, the Man with the Yellow Hat (like a cool, understanding parent figure), in a bustling city.

Their adventures aren't limited to the city; they venture into various locales just like a family might go on trips or outings.

Every episode of the show is like a new day of discovery. George delves into different concepts of science, math, and engineering (imagine a child's first time seeing a rainbow, building a sandcastle, or counting stars). George's curiosity often lands him into tricky situations, much like how a child's inquisitiveness can lead to a spilled vase or a scribbled wall. But with his creative problem-solving and some help from the Man with the Yellow Hat, George always finds a way out, learning important life lessons in the process.

Just as *Curious George* makes learning fun for George, the show does the same for its young audience. It's more than just a TV show, it's a reminder of the joy and wonder of childhood exploration and discovery.

Courageous Curiosity

What if we adopted a childlike and courageous curiosity like George when interacting with people? What if, instead of making presumptions and acting upon biases, we displayed an eager sense of exploration and discovery, just like a child at a new playground, fascinated by every nook, every fellow playmate's unique way of sliding down the slide or swinging on the swing? That's the curiosity we need in our interactions with people, especially those we disagree with.

My friend Hassan Ghiassi brought this idea to life, telling me, "You don't always have to have an opinion before you ask a lot of questions." This brings us to the heart of the matter: asking versus arguing. Imagine a world where our disagreements are filled with questions rather than arguments, where curiosity replaces attacks and callous conflict. Directives like "sit down, shut up, and just listen" rarely yield understanding or progress. However, asking questions sends a different signal—one of openness, interest, and respect.

A 2020 research article lends credibility to this idea, revealing that asking questions can reduce anger and foster positive feelings like those experienced when a conflict is resolved. In essence, curiosity is a peacemaker.[4]

Remember this: it's impossible to stop people from making assumptions. We all do it. The issue lies not in making assumptions, but in accepting them as irrefutable facts. Encouraging curiosity helps us keep our assumptions in check, prompting us to seek more information before we arrive at conclusions.

A valuable lesson that curiosity teaches us is to appreciate the journey that led someone to their beliefs, rather than focusing solely on the beliefs themselves. This kind of curiosity enables us to value the person and their experiences, even if we don't value their viewpoint. It encourages us to see the world through their lens, and in doing so, broadens our own perspective.

Curiosity is more than an attribute; it's a tool for understanding, empathy, and connection. It's the bridge that links diverse minds and helps us navigate the often-tumultuous waters of disagreements. So, let's stay curious and keep asking questions, because it's through curiosity that we learn, grow, connect, and better respectfully disagree.

THE PITFALLS OF SMALL SAMPLE SIZES

Have you ever heard someone argue "but so-and-so said or did this"? Did you wonder when that person was elected to represent their whole demographic? Choosing to cut off curiosity and start or refute an argument based on one or two examples is similar to conducting research with one or two specimens. There's so much variance that it's not a big enough sample size to come to any conclusions.

However, one sample that's always valuable to better understand is your own experience or that of the person you're disagreeing with. Even then, keep in mind that it represents only a singular experience, not that of a whole group. For example, I could tell you that a certain brand of razor I use works best, but that fails to take into account those who can't use razors because of bumps, or those who have a different hair pattern, or those who choose to not buy disposable razors. A few examples should never stifle your curiosity about the person you are disagreeing with.

Imagine you're in a bustling city, filled with all kinds of people. This city is your research population, teeming with diversity and complexity. Now, suppose you want to know what the city dwellers think about a specific topic. Would you ask only a handful of people and assume their views represent everyone? Probably not. This is essentially the challenge when you're dealing with small sample sizes in the context of respectful disagreements and discussions. There are several things to consider when you're tempted to act based on a small sample size:[5]

THE POWER OF REPRESENTATION Say the people you decide to survey are all from the same neighborhood—perhaps they even live on the same street. This is akin to a small sample size. Even though they all reside in the city, their views may not reflect the collective perspective of all the residents. This is the trap of selection bias, similar to cherry-picking viewpoints in a discussion. Recognizing this, you can avoid shaping your arguments based on a narrow lens, ensuring you present a well-rounded perspective.

THE HIDDEN TREASURE Delving deeper into the city analogy, suppose there's a hidden treasure, an insight or truth that reveals itself only when you gather enough clues. With a small sample size, or minimal clues, you might completely miss this treasure. In the realm of respectful disagreement, not considering a wider range of opinions might lead you to miss out on important insights and thus make errors in your arguments.

ACCURACY, THE GUIDING COMPASS If you rely on just a few opinions in the bustling city, your conclusions become less precise, much like navigating through a maze with a faulty compass. In your disagreements and debates, it's essential to minimize this "margin of error" by considering as many perspectives as possible, ensuring your viewpoints are accurate and fair.[6]

THE IMPACT OF OUTLIERS Picture one outspoken individual in the city, someone with views that differ wildly from everyone else's. In a small sample, this person's perspective might skew your overall understanding. Much like in a conversation, one loud, divergent viewpoint should not drown out the multitude of other voices that also deserve to be heard.

THE DISRUPTION OF "THE NORM" Statistical analysis often assumes a "normal" or typical pattern. Small samples, much like a limited viewpoint, can disrupt this assumption. In the city, this could be like assuming everyone enjoys the local sports team's success, while ignoring those who may be indifferent or even disappointed. A truly respectful disagreement involves acknowledging the full range of views, not just those that seem most common or popular.

UNRAVELING COMPLEXITIES The city is a melting pot of perspectives. The relationship between these viewpoints is often complex, and a small sample size might not capture these intricacies. In your journey toward becoming a respectful conversationalist, you learn to appreciate this complexity and avoid oversimplifying your understanding of the issues at hand.

In the cityscape of debate and dialogue, navigating with the map of robust and comprehensive evidence allows us to reach conclusions that are fair, balanced, and insightful. Embracing larger sample sizes helps us cultivate a deeper understanding and appreciation of the diverse perspectives that make our discussions rich and fulfilling. This knowledge strengthens our ability to engage in respectful disagreement, a fundamental cornerstone of constructive conversation.

Simply stated, be courageously curious about others during disagreements because they are adding to your sample size of understanding.

PILLAR 3 RECAP:
CULTIVATE YOUR CURIOSITY

Cultivating curiosity involves nurturing an inquisitive mindset and a desire to explore the unknown. Here's how you can embrace this pillar:

- **Ask questions.** Instead of accepting things at face value, ask questions to deepen your understanding. Challenge assumptions and explore the underlying reasons behind what you encounter.

- **Experiment and explore.** Step out of your comfort zone and try new activities, hobbies, or experiences.

Engaging in unfamiliar endeavors can spark creativity and expand your horizons.

◻ **Stay open-minded and open-hearted.** Embrace uncertainty and be willing to consider alternative perspectives. Approach new ideas or information with a sense of curiosity and a willingness to learn.

REFLECTIONS AND ACTIONS

1. When was the last time you were genuinely curious about something you disagreed with? What was it, why, and what did you learn?

2. Who is one person or what is one group of people that you have taken the exit on, and what is one action you can take to drive toward them?

3. When has someone taken the exit on you? What happened and how did you feel?

CHAPTER 8

Fifty Shades of . . .

Pillar 4, Seek the Gray

This chapter focuses on how you can seek the gray in a society where everything seems to be black and white. Use this chapter to help build dialogues in which you find common ground within your disagreements.

A good while back, I remember a heartbreaking incident involving a young man and a police officer that ended tragically. I was filled with a deep sense of sorrow for the young man's life cut short and the unimaginable grief his family was going through. I felt compelled to share my thoughts on social media, a sort of rallying cry against the injustices happening to young men. Given the like-mindedness of my social media circle at that time, my post was met with plenty of agreement and supportive comments.

However, some responses were overly harsh toward police officers, which made me uncomfortable. Even though I disagreed, I chose to remain silent out of fear of causing a rift. But then, a comment from a young white woman caught my eye. She warned against generalizing all police officers, and I initially reacted with internal defensiveness, saying to myself, *I don't have to be careful on my page.* Instead of lashing out, though, I chose to reach out to her privately to better understand her perspective.

What followed was an eye-opening conversation that changed my entire viewpoint. This woman, whose husband was a police officer, shared their story of serving and living in their community. Her heartfelt story and arguments against broad generalizations made me realize my own mistake. I was guilty of doing exactly what I hated—stereotyping a whole group of people.

This conversation encouraged me to broaden my understanding. I focused on police officers for my own self-titled "circles of grace challenge." I dug deeper by reading articles, speaking to friends in the police force, and asking questions. I even participated in a late-night police ride-along in Charlotte, North Carolina, which added depth to my newfound perspective. I was taken aback by the myriad roles police officers have to play—law enforcer, bodyguard, social worker, mental health counselor, security, and many more (and I experienced this in only three hours).

I began to see police officers not just in the black-and-white extremes I was used to, but in shades of gray. My perception changed. I no longer saw police officers as inherently bad, even though I acknowledged the problematic history of policing toward people of color in the US. I developed a sense of empathy toward them, their training, and what US cities have asked them to do.

It made me ponder how often we see things only in black and white, without appreciating the complexities in between. I'm not perfect (and never will be); there are issues that I still see strictly in black and white, where I have yet to find their gray areas. But each conversation, each interaction, is gradually helping me see the world in a different hue.

What's helping me in this journey is shifting how I see those with opposing views. Instead of seeing them as competitors (something to win against), I'm starting to view them as collaborators (something to explore). It's a powerful exercise in understanding and empathy, because oftentimes our human nature can lead us to simply try winning an argument instead of welcoming dialogue. But instead of seeing only the black and white, we can choose to see a shade of gray. When we seek the gray, we create a space where people feel heard, valued, and maybe even willing to listen to us as well.

Where in your life have you experienced seeing things in just black and white, when there may be more shades of gray to explore?

NOTE Did you notice the gray line on the book's cover? It was created intentionally as a thin line between the black and white, because we have to choose to see it, just as we do for so many things in our world that are portrayed as heavily black and white (politics, territory, LeBron James vs. Michael Jordan, and other very important issues).

COMPETITOR OR COLLABORATOR

As we navigate the journey of life, disagreements are extremely common. The approach we take toward them can make all the difference. Do we view disagreements as something to be won, or as a teamwork challenge that offers an opportunity for collective growth? Many of us might answer,

"Well, it depends," and rightly so. Our stance often depends on our personal connection to the issue or our reaction to recent events that have impacted us.

Competition: The Unending Race

Competing is a part of human nature, and it can drive us toward excellence. We see it on the sports field, in our workplaces, and in our everyday interactions. However, when disagreements emerge and competition takes the front seat, it becomes an unending race where the only goal is to win.

In such a race, we perceive everything in stark black and white. There's a right (our viewpoint) and a wrong (the other person's viewpoint), with no room for the gray areas of consensus or mutual understanding. We listen only to refute and prove the other person wrong, rather than listening to learn and understand.

The satisfaction derived from "winning" this race might seem gratifying in the moment, but it often leaves behind a trail of damaged relationships and resentment.

Collaboration: The Teamwork Challenge

On the other hand, viewing disagreements as an opportunity for collective learning transforms the experience into a teamwork challenge in which all participants work together to solve a problem or accomplish a task. The objective isn't to outdo each other, but to learn from each other's insights and perspectives.

This approach encourages us to respect different viewpoints, viewing them as unique contributions to solve the challenge, not as obstacles to personal victory. The goal here isn't to assert dominance, but to leverage collective intelligence and arrive at an inclusive solution.

You're probably wondering how you can have a team when you're one person. This is a gentle reminder that you can only control yourself, and it is your choice to take a collaborative approach in disagreements. Seeing your conversation as a team effort can help you approach disagreements differently.

Choosing Our Approach

In navigating disagreements, we must aim to turn away from the race and embrace the teamwork challenge. While the race might seem like the path of least resistance at times, it can lead to strained relationships and missed opportunities for growth and understanding. Collaboration, in contrast, fosters understanding, mutual respect, and collective growth.

Respectful disagreement isn't about compromising your viewpoints or blindly accepting the other person's. It's about sharing your perspective while valuing theirs, aiming to solve the challenge in a manner that respects and includes everyone's contribution.

Let's strive to steer away from the competitive race and toward the enriching teamwork challenge. By doing so, we can navigate disagreements in a manner that brings us closer, helping us to respectfully disagree.

THINGS AREN'T ALWAYS WHAT THEY SEEM

When you seek the gray in the black and white, you often find that things aren't what they appear. This is similar to seeing the nuanced nature of a conversation rather than immediately assigning familiar labels. To help you better understand this concept, let's look at a real-life example you might be familiar with.

Several years ago, there was a series of popular commercials from Ameriquest Mortgage with the theme "Don't Judge Too Quickly." One of the commercials shows a man preparing dinner for a romantic evening. He has a pot of red sauce simmering on the stove and is chopping ingredients for the meal. As his back is turned, his cat jumps on the pot and spills the sauce everywhere. He grabs the cat just as his partner walks into the kitchen. She is horrified by what she sees: the man holding a knife in one hand and the red-spattered cat in the other.

In another one of the commercials, a man lies in a hospital bed attended by two doctors. One of the doctors, bothered by a fly, uses the defibrillator paddles to kill it. The fly lands on the man and the doctor leans over and says, "That killed him," just as the man's wife and young daughter walk in the room. The wife and daughter stare in disbelief, the little girl letting go of the balloon she brought her dad, and the commercial abruptly ends.

Each commercial ends with the tagline: "Don't judge too quickly . . . we won't." The humor comes from the stark contrast between what the viewer and the characters in the commercials see and understand. It was a clever way for Ameriquest to promote its business philosophy of not hastily judging their customers' creditworthiness without a thorough examination. However, what I love about the commercials is that they highlight the fact that oftentimes there's more to a situation than meets the eye. Even when things appear to be very black and white, in reality they often have shades of gray, if we choose to see it!

Do you remember a time when you did something wrong and while the circumstance was black and white to others, you understood it to be more gray? Isn't it interesting that it's easier to see the gray in our own lives and situations than it is to see it for others? This is true not just in our personal lives but also in the world around us, even things that have occurred in the past. One example is the Industrial Revolution, which some see as a great thing—a period of progress and prosperity leading to major technological innovations, increased productivity, and improved standards of living for many. On the other hand, it also led to exploitation of workers, environmental degradation, and exacerbated socio-economic inequalities. There are a lot of shades of gray here!

Let's use your beautiful brain as an example. Think back to a time when you believed something to be true, but then as you learned more, you realized it had more gray to it or was more nuanced than you thought. What comes to mind for you? In my own life, there are so many examples of things becoming gray that I'm realizing there's a high probability of more gray ahead of me! This is why I have focused on making progress to shift disagreements from debates to discoveries.

DEBATE OR DISCOVERY

It's a pretty common scene to catch me nudging a teammate to harness the power of disagreement and remember that friction can be the spark for growth. In fact, I mention it so much that I'm thinking about stitching it onto a pillow or making it one of our official company values.

Here's why I'm so sold on this idea. I think a healthy sprinkle of disagreement sharpens us and leads us to stronger solutions. At a glance, debating and discovering might seem like identical twins. But if you take a closer look, you'll find they're more like distant cousins.

When we're in debate mode, we're basically playing dodgeball with questions, trying to knock the other person off-balance rather than really listening or learning. It reminds me of my high school days when I was part of the speech and debate forensics team (not the CSI type of forensics, though that would have been cool, too). We were taught to stay laser-focused on winning, on sticking to our argument like superglue.

Sadly, I feel like this win-or-lose mindset has seeped into just about every corner of society's interactions these days. We're so busy trying to one-up each other that we miss out on a world of discovery. I'm a firm believer that we should trade in our boxing gloves for magnifying glasses, shifting from debating to discovering.

Imagine a world where people aren't just tolerating each other's opinions, but genuinely interested in them. Picture a conversation where two people aren't just waiting for their turn to speak, but sharing their unique perspectives and lighting a spark that forms a completely new idea—something that couldn't have popped up without that initial friction.

Sure, some folks will tell you it's enough to simply nod along politely and act like you're seeing the other person's perspective. But let's be real. That's just playing pretend. What we need is a genuine quest for understanding, not a performance. I'd love to give you an example to bring this idea to life.

The Debating Duo

Once upon a time, in a dynamic city district known as Enlighten Lane, lived an extraordinary couple, Alex and Taylor. They were deeply in love and shared a unique passion: not for travel, gastronomy, or fitness, but for the art of debate. The locals affectionately referred to them as "the debating duo."

Alex was lean, with keen eyes that belied a sharp intellect. Alex's career as a successful corporate lawyer was built on a foundation of logic-driven, factual arguments. Taylor, on the other hand, was an independent author, revered for the ability to blend human experiences with empirical data into captivating narratives.

Their debates began with the sunrise, often over breakfast. "Are avocados overrated?" Taylor would playfully ask, sparking a lively debate that would last well into their morning espressos. The rest of their day would unfold similarly, with one stimulating debate after another, covering topics as diverse as the mysteries of consciousness to the ethical implications of virtual reality.

Their shared loft, affectionately named "The Debatorium," was filled with towering bookshelves, eclectic artifacts, and a multitude of digital resources. Their only ventures outside were to replenish their library, grab a quick meal at a local café, or participate in the occasional city council meeting, where they often commanded attention with their compelling arguments.

However, over time, the couple started to feel the strain of their continuous intellectual sparring. Despite the respect and admiration they held for each other, their relentless quest for the perfect rebuttals began to overshadow the deeper essence of their relationship. The thrill of victory was turning into a source of emotional fatigue, as they found themselves locked in endless loops of disagreement, with no resolution in sight.

Recognizing their dilemma, the city district's renowned thought-leader, Dr. Veritas, invited them to a community forum to debate the purpose of life. This invitation turned into an opportunity for Alex and Taylor to reflect on their interactions and to realize that their passion for debate was slowly eroding the joy in their relationship.

The day of the forum arrived, and the district's residents turned up in full force. Alex and Taylor started the debate, presenting their carefully constructed arguments. However, the repeated cycle of argument and counterargument soon turned into an exhausting whirlwind of words, mirroring the debates that were draining their personal life of its warmth.

Observing their struggle, Dr. Veritas interjected. "Alex, Taylor," she said, her voice filled with calm wisdom, "your relentless pursuit of the perfect rebuttal is driving you apart. Remember, the art of conversation isn't solely about proving a point, but also about discovering and understanding each other's perspectives."

Alex and Taylor fell silent, recognizing the wisdom in Dr. Veritas's words. They had been so focused on their debates that they had overlooked the underlying issue: their need for intellectual victory was stifling their emotional connection and the joy of mutual discovery.

This realization marked a turning point for the duo. They decided to balance their passion for debate with a newfound emphasis on discovery. Debates were no longer seen as battles to be won, but as journeys of mutual learning and understanding. They began spending more time exploring new ideas together, opening their minds to each other's viewpoints rather than focusing solely on refuting them. They even challenged themselves to learn something completely new every year together.

The debating duo became not just better speakers, but also better listeners and learners. Their relationship evolved, strengthening with each discussion, as they discovered the joy of exploring the world of ideas together. This change brought newfound depth and harmony to their relationship, reflecting the wisdom that the heart of conversation lies in discovery and understanding, not just in debate. One amazing way to do this more is with the powerful tool of dialogue.

THE POWER OF DIALOGUE IN RESPECTFUL DISAGREEMENTS

Imagine you're at a family gathering, enjoying a home-cooked meal. Suddenly, a controversial news topic comes up. It's clear you see things differently from your cousin across the table. The room gets tense, but it doesn't have to lead to a blow-up. Disagreements are a natural part of life, and when handled with respectful dialogue, they can open doors to understanding rather than creating walls of division.

The first advantage of dialogue is that it fosters understanding. We each view the world through our unique lenses, shaped by a lifetime of personal experiences. By engaging in dialogue, by truly listening to another's perspective, we gain insight into their world. It's like swapping shoes for a day. This empathetic approach can defuse tension, preventing a disagreement from escalating into a full-blown argument.

Secondly, dialogue is a powerful learning tool. Ever had a sudden realization in the middle of a conversation? That's the magic of dialogue. When we engage in dialogue about a disagreement, we expose ourselves to new viewpoints, like reading a new chapter of a book. It broadens our perspectives, sometimes nudging us to reconsider our own stance.

The third virtue of dialogue is problem-solving. Disagreements often revolve around tangible issues that require solutions. Think of a dialogue as laying all the puzzle pieces on the table. Together, you can examine each piece, gaining a clearer picture of the problem and enabling a solution that considers everyone's viewpoint.

Moreover, engaging in dialogue is a testament to respect and acknowledges the dignity of others. Remember the Golden Rule: treat others as you wish to be treated. When you invite someone into dialogue and listen attentively to their viewpoint, you're saying, "I respect you and value your perspective." This simple act can humanize the situation, reducing the risk of hurt feelings and possibly fostering a sense of safety.

Lastly, and perhaps surprisingly, dialogue during disagreements can bring us closer together. It's akin to surviving an adventure with a friend—you encounter obstacles, but the shared experience strengthens your bond. When you're open and honest in your dialogue, it signals trust and vulnerability, which can enhance relationships, even when you're arguing over something.[1]

A thoughtful, respectful dialogue is an invaluable tool when handling disagreements. It helps us to understand, learn, problem-solve, show respect, and even build relationships. By remembering to open a dialogue instead of resorting to heated debates, we can transform our disagreements into opportunities for growth and connection.

During my MBA program, a professor recommended one of the best books I have ever read on how to have meaningful conversations: William Isaacs's *Dialogue: The Art of Thinking Together*.[2] It is often considered a seminal work in the field of organizational communication and dialogue studies. These are the core principles outlined by Isaacs:

- **Listening.** Listening is not simply about being quiet while the other person talks, it's about truly understanding and reflecting on the speaker's point of view. This involves the idea of *generative listening*, where one listens not merely to understand but also to help the speaker articulate their perspective.

- **Respecting.** Every individual involved in the dialogue should feel valued and respected. Each person's opinion matters, and everyone has something unique to contribute to the discussion.

◘ **Suspending.** This involves holding back one's reactions, judgments, or preconceived notions to fully comprehend the other person's point of view. It allows individuals to see the assumptions and biases that may be influencing their thoughts and reactions.

◘ **Voicing.** Each person should feel free to voice their ideas, thoughts, and feelings without fear of ridicule or judgment. The process of voicing allows for the emergence of new insights and understanding.

◘ **Participating.** Everyone should participate actively in the dialogue. This fosters a sense of belonging and equality among all participants.

◘ **Inquiring and reflecting.** Dialogue is not simply about sharing ideas, it also involves inquiring deeply into the subject matter, reflecting on it, and constantly learning from the process.

Isaacs sums it all up in one simple point: true dialogue is not about one person trying to convince the other of A and the other person trying to convince the first of B, but rather about how they can create C together. C isn't necessarily a 50/50 combination; it could be 60/40, 25/75, or even 98/2. This is the essence of finding the gray rather than only the black and white!

When we see others as collaborators rather than competitors, and when we are intentional in seeking the gray in the black and white, we can humanize our disagreement partner. We also create a space where more respectful disagreement can thrive.

PILLAR 4 RECAP:
SEEK THE GRAY

Seeking the gray is about embracing complexity and recognizing that the world is not always black and white. Here's how you can practice this pillar:

◻ **Seek nuance.** Avoid simplistic binary thinking and strive to understand the intricacies of any given situation. Consider multiple factors and perspectives before forming judgments or making decisions.

◻ **Embrace ambiguity.** Be comfortable with uncertainty and learn to navigate through situations where clear-cut answers may not exist. Practice patience and allow space for ambiguity in your decision-making process.

REFLECTIONS AND ACTIONS

1. What is one example where you initially viewed something as black and white but later saw the gray?

2. Are you more of a debater or a discoverer? Why do you think you are that way?

3. Which of the six core principles by William Isaacs stood out the most to you and why?

CHAPTER 9

A Path Forward

Pillar 5, Agree to Respect

n this chapter you'll learn some practical ways to respect others by fully acknowledging them. Use this chapter to apply the 3FA model and "Thank You, Because" as tools to respect others when disagreeing.

In the tapestry of humanity, there are few true stories as intriguing and complex as those of redemption and transformation. I found one such story in an unlikely place, nested within the coarse, hardened life of a former colleague of mine, an ex-skinhead I'll call Jack (not his real name).

Jack's past was rife with hate and prejudice. He was a man feared in the streets, despised in society, and yet he stood unapologetically tall. He wore his views like armor, hardened over the years by the hail of criticism and social disdain. Jack reveled in the derogatory labels he received; terms like *racist* and *misogynist* seemed to feed his sense of identity. He laughed at them with a scornful chuckle. Each denouncement, each shout, each yell served only to fuel his fervor, to deepen his commitment to his cause. It was a vicious cycle, where his hate thrived on their loathing, and their loathing amplified his hate.

Jack became this way from years of neglect and physical abuse. His dad, after finishing work at the local plant, would get drunk and take out his anger on Jack. He not only blamed Jack for a myriad of things but also constantly complained that "outsiders" were responsible for the wrong direction of the country. Jack internalized this message and the horrid abuse, leading him to look for belonging and a community wherever he could find it. He didn't fully believe in the hate he spread to others, but having a welcoming community was more important to him than the message. Desperately wanting a connection with his dad, Jack connected with those who shared views similar to his dad's.

I was extremely intrigued by Jack's transformation, so I asked him what the catalyst for change was. Having assumed it was something like a heartfelt conversation with a family member or a deep-dive counseling session, I was baffled by Jack's response. You see, confrontation was Jack's sustenance, his distorted source of validation. It was an addictive cocktail of adrenaline, righteous indignation, and distorted pride. The world was a battlefield, and everyone who wasn't with him was his enemy. And it seemed like Jack would remain rooted in his bigoted stance, seemingly impervious to change.

But then came the seeds of transformation.

In a world filled with angry voices, there were a few who chose to tread a different path. These people he demeaned and marginalized didn't shout or yell. Instead, they dared to listen, to understand. They heard his story without interrupting, without letting their own beliefs cast a judgmental shadow. They chose to be open-hearted toward Jack while still closing off their minds to his hate speech. They extended to Jack something he had never expected: respect.

It was these quiet, persistent voices that made Jack pause. They were the ones he demeaned, the ones he hated, and yet they met his venom with kindness, his hostility with patience. They refused to echo his bitterness, choosing instead to treat him with dignity, offering him a sense of humanity he had forgotten he was capable of receiving.

In their unwavering show of respect, Jack found a disquieting question: How could he hate those who refused to hate him in return? The paradox gnawed at him, a splinter in his once unshakeable armor of conviction. He found himself questioning the basis of his prejudices, the rationale for his hostility.

The mirror they held up to him was not one of disrespect or hatred but of understanding and empathy. And it was this reflection of a potential self—one not defined by hate but capable of respect and dignity—that made Jack confront the man he had become.

In their choice to respect, he found the strength to start dismantling the wall of prejudice he had built. He acknowledged their care, their value, and most importantly, their dignity. It was a grueling journey, filled with introspection, remorse, and painful realizations. But it was a path that led him away from the mire of hatred and toward the light of acceptance and respect.

It's a tragic irony that many of these compassionate individuals may never realize the profound impact they had on Jack's life. They saw in him what he couldn't see in himself, and it was their faith in his capacity for change that eventually bridged the vast divide of hate. It is a potent reminder that even in the face of prejudice, the choice to respond with empathy and respect can plant the seeds for unimaginable transformation.

Jack's story, a true one, is not just a tale of personal redemption but also a lesson about the power of transformation and respect. It teaches us that the strongest catalyst for change is conscious compassion rather than callous confrontation. And this change, this redemption, is not only possible but within reach for those who dare to extend the hand of respect. While the people Jack hated are clearly not responsible for his growth as a human, they planted seeds that he could no longer ignore.

HOW YOU START MATTERS

It's often challenging to separate a person from their views, especially when the person exists outside of our circles of grace—the group of individuals we naturally empathize with. This lack of separation escalates disagreements, turning civil discourse into personal contempt. As a 2008 research article put it: "Animosity for a person's position becomes contempt for the person."[1] This makes it even more important to start disagreements in the best way possible.

The first signs of discord often signal a conversation spiraling out of control.[2] Thus, how you start a disagreement significantly impacts its trajectory and possible resolution. A lack of conversational receptiveness (acknowledgment and listening) at the beginning of a conversation can increase the chances of conflict escalation.

In addition, as a 2017 study concluded, the mode of communication can affect how we perceive disagreements.[3] The researchers found that we humanize people more when we hear their voice rather than reading their words; specifically, evaluators were better persuaded when they heard the voice of the person they disagreed with rather than reading the same words. Voice, it seems, adds a humanizing element that makes us more open to engaging with opposing views. This suggests that direct, voiced communication might be a key ingredient in creating understanding and finding common ground.

However, it's important to remember that the goal here is awareness, not perfection. I don't expect you to become a flawless communicator overnight. Instead, we can focus on creating the right environment for respectful disagreements. As an example, introducing alcohol into the mix can be counterproductive because it often blunts our receptiveness and heightens negative emotional responses.

Another crucial aspect to respectful disagreements is how we choose to share our perspective. Two crucial elements come into play in laying the groundwork for productive disagreements: vulnerability and humility. By opening up about our own uncertainties and recognizing that we don't have all the answers, we create an environment that encourages mutual exploration rather than defensive standoffs. Moreover, disagreements are most productive when underpinned by a foundation of trust and a shared purpose.

But it's not just about emotional preparedness. Our physical state also influences how well we handle disagreements. Are we well fed? Rested? Not already aggravated by an unrelated issue? Do we feel physically safe? These questions may seem trivial, but they play a significant role in our ability to respectfully disagree. These are also good things to consider for the person on the other side of the argument. It's important to do a "self check-in" before engaging in a disagreement.

Sometimes, it may also be necessary to break down a disagreement into a series of conversations rather than trying to resolve it in one sitting. Giving everyone time to process and reflect can often lead to more thoughtful responses and less reactive arguments.

In conclusion, approach conversations and disagreements as a drummer in a drum circle would, not as a soldier going to war. Choose your engagements carefully and always work toward harmony. Each conversational beat you add should aim to enhance the rhythm of understanding, not drown out the beats of others. In this way, we can encourage ourselves and others to bring our best selves to the conversation table.

RECEPTIVENESS RECIPE

Can you recall a moment when you sat across from someone with every fiber of your being yearning to lash out, to verbalize the raw anger simmering just beneath your skin? Now, imagine if instead of anger, you chose curiosity. This was the dilemma I faced while listening to my father's account, a story that had the power to evoke such a tremendous response from me. But the true challenge isn't just swallowing the fury, it's also about refraining from placing the weight of our assumptions on their intent. How about you? How do you react when faced with the high stakes of a challenging conversation?

I want to revisit the concept of conversational receptiveness—a term that holds an ocean of potential in the way we communicate, especially when it involves conflicting views. Simply put, conversational receptiveness is the willingness to consider another's perspective, even when it clashes with our own, fostering an atmosphere of understanding and evaluation rather than outright denial.[4]

An enlightening article from *Harvard Business Review*, "Disagreement Doesn't Have to Be Divisive," offers four key strategies to cultivate conversational receptiveness:

- Acknowledge the other person's perspective. A simple expression of gratitude can go a long way: "Thank you so much for sharing your perspective with me."

- Express your claims with a dash of uncertainty, embracing a less dogmatic approach: "There may be some truth to that point."

- Frame your disagreements positively. Consider an abundance mindset over a deficit mindset: "Isn't it great that we can disagree respectfully on this issue?"

- Highlight even the smallest areas of agreement. Passionate disagreement does not invalidate shared values, common beliefs, or common ground: "I am glad that we are both after the safety of our children."[5]

In an intriguing revelation, a study described in the article found that people embracing this "receptiveness recipe" were seen not only as desirable collaborators but also as more persuasive messengers. Furthermore, the article suggests using "I" statements instead of "you" statements, which tend to feel accusatory. By saying, "I feel hurt when you cut me off" rather than "You disrespect me when you cut me off," you help maintain a nonconfrontational atmosphere.

The path to becoming more receptive might be laden with challenges, yet with intentionality, it's a skill that can be honed. A simple strategy is the use of softeners like *somewhat*, *might*, and *possible* to mitigate the harshness of your statements. This is what it means to "hedge your claims," akin to a scientific researcher's cautious approach to stating results.

An interesting study on Wikipedia editors further illustrates the power of conversational receptiveness. The researchers found that editors who communicated receptively were less likely to be subjected to personal attacks, emphasizing how such an approach can shield discussions from escalating into heated conflicts.[6]

At the heart of all this research is a fundamental truth: we have the ability to acknowledge the other party, no matter how strongly we disagree with them. In doing so, we recognize their humanity, creating a space where open, honest, and respectful communication can thrive.

Culture and Receptiveness

As shared in chapter 2, I have found that learning from other cultures can sometimes inform how to better respect others. Every culture has different ways to show receptiveness while disagreeing with others, and it is important to filter this material not as a one-size-fits-all approach, but instead as a helpful guide in your journey. Here is an example based on a traditional Chinese workplace.

You are meeting with your boss, Mr. Li, who has just proposed a new marketing strategy.

Disrespectful Disagreement

Mr. Li: *"I believe we should focus on improving our brand awareness."*

You (rolling your eyes and crossing your arms): *"Mr. Li, do you really think that would work?"*
Without waiting for his response, you continue in a dismissive tone.

You: *"That makes no sense. What if the market doesn't respond well? You didn't think about that at all with this idea."*
You then lean back in your chair, signaling a lack of interest in further discussion or collaboration.

This behavior is generally seen as very disrespectful in Chinese culture. The manner of speaking, body language, and lack of consideration for Mr. Li's position and face are likely to create conflict and harm relationships in the work-place. In many cultures, including Chinese culture, it's considered very important to express disagreement or criticism in what might be considered a constructive and indirect way.

Respectful Disagreement

Mr. Li: "I believe we should focus on improving our brand awareness."

You (nodding and maintaining respectful eye contact): "Hello, Mr. Li. I have given careful thought to your perspective. The strategy of improving brand awareness indeed has its unique aspects, which impresses me."
You pause for a moment, letting your acknowledgment of his idea sink in.

You (with a thoughtful expression): "However, I also have some different views on this. Have we considered what might happen if the market reaction is not as enthusiastic as we expect?"
You give Mr. Li a moment to consider your question before continuing.

You (proposing a solution): "I think if we could add some safeguards to the existing strategy, our plan might be more secure. I look forward to your thoughts on this to find the best solution."

You might end your statement with a respectful slight bow, signaling your intention to maintain harmony and collaborate on the issue.

This example demonstrates respectful disagreement within the context of a traditional Chinese workplace. It shows how to address the issue indirectly while preserving the respect and face of the person you are disagreeing with.

Your demeanor, body language, and tone of voice are just as important as your words in this context. If you review this example closely, you'll see it overlaps the research on conversational receptiveness.

ACKNOWLEDGING ALWAYS

I have often heard others say, "Let's just agree to disagree," and while I understand the sentiment, let me push back on the statement. Some people use this as a way to get out of the argument. One thing I've learned is that you can agree to disagree *disrespectfully*, which is exactly what we're challenging. What we can agree on is to acknowledge others in our disagreements. We can agree to ask them for their perspective. We can agree to express common ground.

What if we listened to others as if they could actually teach us something? This simple yet profound question has the potential to transform how we communicate, particularly in challenging dialogues and disagreements. Perhaps it sounds lofty or even slightly impractical. After all, we're all human, and it's only natural to falter in our quest for perfect communication. But by consistently reminding ourselves of this principle before entering difficult conversations, we can cultivate a more open and receptive mindset.

3FA Framework

To successfully bridge conversational divides, we must remember to acknowledge the other party, even in instances of significant disagreement. Acknowledgment can be as simple as expressing gratitude for their contribution to the conversation. This concept led my team and I to develop the

3FA Framework, a practical tool for acknowledgment that embodies the power we all possess to affirm others.

There are three types of Full Acknowledgment (FA) in this framework:

- **FA+FA: Full Acknowledgment, Full Agreement.**
  This is when we find ourselves completely agreeing with the other party. We can express this by saying something like, "I agree 100 percent with you."

- **FA+PA: Full Acknowledgment, Partial Agreement.**
  There are instances where we might not fully agree with someone, but we find certain points of their argument compelling. In such cases, we might say, "While I don't fully agree with you, I definitely agree with what you said about X."

- **FA+NA: Full Acknowledgment, No Agreement.**
  Even when there is no agreement, there is always room for acknowledgment. You can communicate this by saying, "Thank you so much for sharing your perspective with me."

Other phrases can help foster acknowledgment, too, such as "I understand that," "I appreciate you for sharing your perspective," or "I feel you when you say X."

At this point, it's crucial to dispel a common misconception: many individuals hesitate to acknowledge others because they fear it's equivalent to capitulating to or losing an argument. This perspective often arises from viewing disagreements as competitive or zero-sum scenarios. However, we must remember that respectful disagreement is not a contest. Acknowledgment does not necessarily equate to agreement. It's a show of respect and understanding, a nod to the individual's courage to express their opinion. And for that, we can always say thank you.

Thank You, Because

Growing up, my mother instilled in me the importance of basic courtesies, most notably saying "please" and "thank you." While these fundamental lessons have stood the test of time, I often wonder if there's an unexplored facet to this courtesy. What if we could enhance our conversations and disagreements by simply appending "because" to our thank yous?

This novel approach to acknowledgment was developed by Stanford researcher Xuan Zhao and inspired by the improv game of "Yes, and." In her exploration of effective conversational techniques, Zhao identified three key methods: "Thank you, because"; "I hear that, and"; and "No, because." She found that we often default to "No, because" in disagreements, focusing on identifying faults and refuting the other person's viewpoints.[7]

However, in her research, Zhao discovered that employing the "Thank you, because" technique resulted in more inclusive conversations. Participants reported feeling heard and an increased perception of common ground. This approach of expressing affirmation or appreciation, even amid disagreements, was found to foster respectful dialogues. Such a method isn't a sign of weakness; on the contrary, it exemplifies strength and respect.

Disagreements are not battles to be won; they are opportunities to understand and grow. If we approach them with a combative mindset, we risk missing the potential insights they could offer. Instead, consider emulating sports figures who value sportsmanship over sheer victory, treating their opponents with respect and dignity. This reminds me of the story of the 10K race in Thailand. One athlete fell to the track in utter exhaustion near the finish line. While other runners kept running, one sacrificed his own race to help his fallen "competitor." This act of humanity is something to consider emulating in the realm of respectful disagreement.[8]

The "Thank you, because" approach is about appreciating the value in another's viewpoint, even if you disagree with it. You might thank them for their courage to share, or perhaps you can find common ground in their argument. For instance, during a debate on wearing masks, you could affirm, "Thank you, because we both agree that we can't wait for this pandemic to be over!" Such an approach promotes affirming behaviors, leading to more cooperative dialogues and better impressions of the other party.

Zhao's research indicates that using "Thank you, because" helps individuals feel valued and heard and see the conversation as more collaborative. It tends to be slightly more effective than "I hear that," as it not only acknowledges the other party's viewpoint but also establishes common ground. Acknowledging others using "Thank you, because" is one way to respectfully disagree and humanize others.

In contrast, the "No, because" approach focuses on finding fault in the other person's reasoning. It often involves dissecting each statement, identifying their incoherent logic or misinformed facts, to demonstrate why their position warrants rejection. This combative approach might seem satisfying in the short term, but it's inefficient and rarely leads to positive change.

What if we could feel good about ourselves while inspiring others to feel good about themselves too? By embracing the "Thank you, because" approach, we can foster a culture of respect, affirmation, and mutual growth in our conversations.

HOW WE CHOOSE TO COMMUNICATE

What we say and how we say it matters to respectful disagreement. Consider this example: I've never been a big fan of tattoos. Now, if I were to express this sentiment, I could ask someone, "Why would you get a tattoo?" or I could ask, "What inspired you to get a tattoo?" They're essentially the same question, but with vastly different connotations. The choice of words, and the medium used to convey these words, profoundly impacts the tone and outcome of the conversation.

One area of concern is where we choose to communicate our disagreement. No, I'm not talking about picking out restaurants or your favorite coffee shop, but rather communicating through text and online forums, chats, and comment sections. These places have produced some of the most misunderstood and misinterpreted disagreements that consistently escalate to disrespectful. It's time to rethink where we disagree with others if we want to communicate respectfully.

Remember the Golden Rule? "Treat others the way you want to be treated." And the Platinum Rule? "Treat others the way they want to be treated." One of the simplest ways to uphold these rules, particularly in disagreements, is through our choice of communication medium. Studies on written, spoken, and in-person communication show that our choice of medium can significantly affect the nature of difficult conversations and our efforts to humanize others. For instance, people generally prefer to write about ideological differences rather than speak them out loud. However, speaking directly with the "other" has been found to enhance the humanization of others, reduce conflict, and foster understanding and mutual respect.[9]

Online communication, due to its relative anonymity, often breeds antagonism and aggression. Yet the written form also provides ample time for thought composition, leading to more articulate and intelligent responses than impromptu speech. Interestingly, hearing someone's opinion rather than reading it tends to humanize the communicator, making them appear more intelligent. Thus, restricting disagreements to written forms deprives us of the opportunity to humanize others. This highlights the importance of choosing the right medium for productive disagreement.

Why, then, don't more people pick up the phone to hash out disagreements? The answer lies in the perceived intellectual satisfaction of written communication. The luxury of time to compose one's thoughts often leads people to favor written forms such as texts, emails, direct messages, and online forums. However, listening to others' spoken words gives us a more accurate understanding of their thoughts and feelings. Tactics aimed at winning the conversation can inhibit the parties involved from bringing their best to the discussion. Research has shown that online communication's lack of nonverbal cues (inflection, body language, etc.) often leads to misinterpretations and disagreements.[10]

So what about face-to-face communication? Which medium do you think is most effective for respectful disagreement—written, voice, or face-to-face (online or in person)? While you might intuitively pick the third option, research suggests otherwise. Visual cues, once voice interaction is established, do not significantly alter our impressions of others. This insight reduces the need for in-person meetings or online video chats, making a simple phone call a sufficient means of communicating disagreement. This might differ from person to person, so please be open. For example, if you are engaging someone who is deaf or hard of hearing, facial clues may be vital to a respectful disagreement.

By choosing to write (or type) rather than speak, we often prioritize self-interest over optimal outcomes. Nevertheless, writing can be a useful tool when used in conjunction with spoken dialogue.

Research supports this viewpoint, with multiple experiments revealing that spoken conversations promote more humanization and civility than written exchanges. In a surprising finding, speaking to another person—rather than seeing them—had a similar humanizing effect. Asynchronous spoken conversations (like voice memos) had similar effects as both written asynchronous and synchronous dialogues.[11] This reaffirms that our choice of medium matters significantly in facilitating respectful disagreements and humanizing one another.

SHARING IS CARING

You've probably read up to this point and are wondering: Should I ever share? Is my sharing humanizing or dehumanizing? Well, the answer to that question isn't black and white (seek the gray!). It depends largely on how and why you share. The focus of your sharing determines whether it enriches the conversation or stifles it. Are you merely venting, or are you genuinely seeking a constructive outcome?

There are moments when we just want to let off some steam, to empty the cauldron of our thoughts that has been simmering for too long. In such cases, having a supportive group where we can freely express ourselves is a blessing. However, it's important not to confuse this cathartic release with constructive conversations. More often than not, a mind clouded with emotions is unlikely to find the most effective solution and can inadvertently complicate matters further. So, it's essential to ask yourself: What's your ultimate goal when sharing your perspective? Your answer will greatly influence whether the following suggestions will be beneficial to you.

Consider this: What if, before you shared your perspective, you asked for permission to do so? It might sound counterintuitive in our outspoken culture, but this simple act of courtesy can pave the way for a deeper connection and more respectful exchange. Now, you might be thinking, *What if they decline?* Well, in that case, your words would have likely fallen on unwilling ears, rendering the exchange futile. I often find that I'm operating from the Superior Self and ego when I don't want to fathom asking, "Are you okay with me sharing my perspective?"

In the few instances where someone says no, it's important to be gracious, respectful, and patient. Leave the door ajar by saying, "If you ever feel open to hearing my perspective, let me know. I would love to share it with you." This respectful approach allows them to choose to engage with your viewpoint when they are ready. You may argue, "But they didn't ask for my consent before sharing their perspective!" Remember, we only have control over our actions and reactions, not others'.

Let me introduce you to a tool my colleagues and I refer to as the "QS Method"—a question and a statement that are particularly useful when you're giving feedback on someone else's point of view. First, politely ask for their consent to provide your feedback (Question). Follow this by communicating that they had the best intentions possible when they shared their views (Statement). This gentle, respectful approach nudges them to open up to your perspective instead of feeling like it's being forced upon them.

It looks something like:

Q: Do you mind if I share my view on what you shared?
(They respond.)

S: I realize that you likely meant the absolute best when you said X, but this is how it came across to me.

Such an exchange doesn't merely promote communication; it fosters a more humanizing interaction. We remember that behind each perspective is a person, with their unique experiences and understanding. This mindful sharing can make all the difference, enhancing the quality of our interactions and enriching our collective perspectives.

In your disagreements, what will be your plan to humanize the other person? What's your first step forward?

PILLAR 5 RECAP: AGREE TO RESPECT

Respect is essential in fostering positive relationships and creating a harmonious environment. Here's how you can incorporate this pillar into your life:

- **Fully acknowledge others.** Acknowledge those you disagree with and thank them for sharing their view, even if it differs from your own. Treat everyone with kindness, empathy, and respect.

- **Embrace diversity and inclusion.** Value and appreciate the uniqueness of individuals from different backgrounds, cultures, and beliefs. Create an inclusive environment by first asking what it looks like for each person when they feel respected and valued.

REFLECTIONS AND ACTIONS

1. What do you think are the benefits of the 3FA Framework in respectful disagreements?

2. How do you think using "Thank you, because" can help people feel seen, valued, and heard? Have you experienced someone using this with you?

3. In what ways do you think assuming positive intent is best in challenging conversations?

CHAPTER 10

What Do I Do Now?

A Call to Meaningful Action

T his is the last chapter, but not the end of this work. This is a "Where do we go from here?" chapter. Please use it as inspiration as you decide what to do next to progress toward having more respectful disagreements.

Are you familiar with the remarkable concept of the Human Library? If you're not, let me usher you into its intriguing world.

Conceived in Denmark in 2000, the Human Library is a metaphorical library that strives to initiate dialogues to break stereotypes and overcome prejudices. It's based on the ingenious premise that just as a traditional library holds a multitude of stories, humans, too, are the custodians of diverse narratives and life experiences.

In the Human Library, individuals become "books," available to be "borrowed" by others interested in their unique stories. The objective? To kindle understanding and empathy among people from disparate backgrounds and experiences. The books you can explore cover a wide spectrum of life situations and subjects, from Alcoholic and Autism to Bipolar and Body Mod Extreme; from Muslim to Naturist and Polyamorous. The essence of this library is to "unjudge" someone by actively engaging in their life narrative.[1]

Having spread its roots across more than eighty countries, the Human Library also features a Book of the Month, such as the Holocaust Survivor or the Transformista. The selection of books at each event is inherently dynamic, varying according to local contexts and the individuals who step forward to share their stories.

Every Human Library event is designed to create a safe and comfortable environment for both the books and the readers. As a reader, you're encouraged to ask questions, fostering a space for intimate, candid, and honest conversation. This setting aids in dismantling barriers and challenging preconceived notions.

What I find compelling about this concept is how it provides an active approach to humanizing others, simply by listening to their stories. Every narrative is distinct, and this powerful act has broadened my perspective, enabling me to recognize and appreciate people for who they truly are. While I have not yet participated in an actual Human Library event, I have listened to stories of people I did not know a lot about and even those I actively disagree with. Although I haven't always agreed with the perspectives I've encountered, it has reinforced the idea that regardless of our disagreements, we must respect each other's humanity.

Be warned: this process isn't flawless. Sometimes, we might find ourselves faltering, and at times, disagreeing disrespectfully and sometimes even disrespectfully agreeing. If you find yourself in such a situation, let's navigate this journey together.

WHERE DO YOU START?

Whew! You made it to the last chapter of the book, and I am so thankful for you. With all the information, stories, research, and corny jokes shared, you might feel a little overwhelmed and wonder how you can put this into practice. I am right there with you. I know it can feel like a lot to do, but remember it's about choosing small, consistent actions (the Tortoise Principle) to make long-lasting change in your life. Next, I want to provide you with some potential ways to move forward:

1. Share two or three key insights from the book with someone you are close to. This is important because you can't do everything at once, but when you talk about it with someone else, it begins to cement the ideas and actions in your heart and head. When sharing these insights, explain why they stood out to you and one thing you plan on doing differently based on this book.

2. Start right where you are with people you love and trust. Sometimes the best place to begin something new is with people who support you and want to see you succeed. Share with someone that you read a book by this bald guy, and you are learning to have more respectful disagreements. If they look at you with disbelief, let them know you will need their help in your growth process. After you have had a few rounds with people you love and trust, try it out in spaces outside of your inner circle. Remember you won't be perfect and you'll make mistakes, but it's a part of your learning and progress forward.

3. Take the Choose Your Own Circles of Grace Challenge. Pick a topic or group of people that you disagree with and intentionally learn about them. Over a three-to-six-month period (or whatever you choose)

go to events, participate in experiences, and engage with people that you disagree with and learn as much as you can. At the end of this challenge, ask yourself two questions: (1) What did I learn about this group of people or ideology? (2) What did I learn about myself as I experienced them? You might consider attending a Human Library event or something like it (and maybe even starting your own).

4. Take the No Disagreement Challenge. Try to avoid disagreeing with others for a day (or, for the very ambitious, a few days) and instead focus on asking thoughtful questions and fully acknowledging those around you. If your role or circumstances compel you to voice your dissenting opinion, make it a rule to ask at least three questions (the Power of 3) before presenting your viewpoint, and use qualifying language to "hedge" your claims (e.g., "This could be helpful," or "It's possible that . . ."). Make sure you keep applying Golden Respect. If you mess up, apologize and work toward bridging the divide again. Consider maintaining a journal to note your feelings and experiences during this period. For some of you, a single day might be enough to realize the frequency and nature of your disagreements with others. It's all right if you don't execute this perfectly; the key objective from the start is progressive improvement.

Bonus: Identify a recent disagreement where you either disrespectfully disagreed or disrespectfully agreed, and apologize. Again, start with people you know, love, and trust for this. Ask to hear more of their view and perspective and apply the 5 Pillars of Bridging the Divide. If you struggle with an area, come back to this book (or identify other books) that can help you dive deeper to achieve meaningful growth.

WHAT TO DO IF YOU'VE GONE ASTRAY

As we prepared for an impending major hiking expedition, a close friend and I talked on the phone, debating the attendees. His focus appeared to be the number of women versus men, and I was left wondering why this factor was so important to him. His explanation related to respect for his wife: he preferred a higher male to female ratio so that, as he put it, "there would not be a perception problem."

His sentiment struck me as puzzling, largely because it contrasted with my own experiences. Recollections from my last journey to Mount Kilimanjaro, where women were in the majority, flashed before me. It had never struck me as a significant factor. I boldly stated that a trusting relationship wouldn't be swayed by such trivialities, impulsively labeling his concern as senseless. (I ask you to refrain from passing judgment on me at this juncture!)

Yes, it was ironic given that I spend considerable time educating others about respectful disagreement, yet I was belittling something my friend considered important. He rebuffed me, standing his ground, declaring that his approach was not foolish but respectful, adding that anyone with a significant other would care about perceived impressions. His retort served as a mirror, reflecting the negativity in my approach, and I was startled to see what I had done. I had dismissed his perspective simply because it didn't align with mine.

Recognizing my blunder, I quickly offered an apology for my thoughtless remark. I acknowledged that he had every right to prioritize his relationship as he saw fit, and conceded that I had been in the wrong. Where my narrow mindset and ill-chosen words had erected barriers, my apology built a bridge to mend the divide.

None of us can claim to be flawless; we are all susceptible to error. But the key lies in our readiness to make amends when we err. I can't claim pride in my handling of that disagreement, yet I remain grateful for the power vested in the simple phrase "I apologize." If uttered sincerely, it's the first step to bridge a divide when matters veer off course. My remorse was genuine, not the result of a PR agency's scripted words to appease societal expectations, but an honest realization of my misstep. While I still hold divergent views regarding the gender ratio's significance, I respect its importance to him and acknowledge how I could have responded more considerately.

Now, the choice lies before us: to uphold respect or succumb to disrespect. Each moment offers us this choice. Even if we falter and stumble below the respect line, the route to ascend lies within the 5 Pillars. Bear in mind, this isn't about validating others' beliefs but about acknowledging their humanity!

REFLECTIONS AND ACTIONS

1. What is one thing that you will do differently after reading this book?

2. With the Circles of Grace Challenge, what group would you start with and why?

3. If you decided to take the No Disagreement Challenge, which duration would you select and why?

NOTES

1 Pew Research Center, "Political Parties & Polarization," accessed August 9, 2022, *https://www.pewresearch.org/topic/politics-policy /political-parties-polarization/*.

2 United Nations, "With Highest Number of Violent Conflicts since Second World War, United Nations Must Rethink Efforts to Achieve, Sustain Peace, Speakers Tell Security Council," news release SC/15184, January 26, 2023, *https://press.un.org/en/2023 /sc15184.doc.htm*.

3 United Nations, "Violence, Insecurity and Climate Change Drive 84 Million People from Their Homes," November 11, 2023, *https:// news.un.org/en/story/2021/11/1105592*.

4 Michael Yeomans et al., "Conversational Receptiveness: Improving Engagement with Opposing Views," *Organizational Behavior and Human Decision Processes* 160 (2020): 132, *https://doi.org/10.1016 /j.obhdp.2020.03.011*.

5 Justin Jones-Fosu, *The Inclusive Mindset: How to Cultivate Diversity in Your Everyday Life* (Charlotte, NC: Peter Jones Publishing, 2021).

CHAPTER 1

1 The Arbinger Institute, *The Anatomy of Peace: Resolving the Heart of Conflict*, 4th ed. (Oakland, CA: Berrett-Koehler, 2022).

2 Michael Yeomans et al., "Conversational Receptiveness: Improving Engagement with Opposing Views," *Organizational Behavior and Human Decision Processes* 160 (2020): 131, *https://doi.org/10.1016 /j.obhdp.2020.03.011*.

3 Jeremy A. Frimer, Linda J. Skitka, and Matt Motyl, "Liberals and Conservatives Are Similarly Motivated to Avoid Exposure to One Another's Opinions," *Journal of Experimental Social Psychology* 72 (2017): 1–12, *https://doi.org/10.1016/j.jesp.2017.04.003.*

CHAPTER 2

1 "French and Raven's Bases of Power," Wikipedia, April 10, 2023, *https://en.wikipedia.org/wiki/French_and_Raven%27s_bases_of_power.*

2 John Gottman and Julie Gottman, "The Natural Principles of Love," *Journal of Family Theory and Review* 9 (2017): 7–26, *https://doi.org/10.1111/jftr.12182*

3 Robert A. Rohm, "A Powerful Way to Understand People Using the DISC Concept," accessed October 11, 2023, *https://www.discoveryreport.com/downloads/understanding-people-disc-personality-traits.pdf*

4 Viktor E. Frankl, Harold S. Kushner, and William J. Winslade, *Man's Search for Meaning* (Boston: Beacon Press, 2006).

5 Reuters Staff, "A Picture and Its Story: Black Man Carries Suspected Far-Right Protester to Safety," Reuters, June 14, 2020, *https://www.reuters.com/article/uk-minneapolis-police-protests-britain-i-idUKKBN23L0W5.*

6 Frankl et al., *Man's Search for Meaning.*

7 Budget Direct, "Cats vs. Dogs: Which Does the World Prefer?," Insurance Solved Blog, December 10, 2021, *https://www.budgetdirect.com.au/blog/cats-vs-dogs-which-does-the-world-prefer.html*; American Veterinary Medical Association, "U.S. Pet Ownership Statistics," accessed September 1, 2023, *https://www.avma.org/resources-tools/reports-statistics/us-pet-ownership-statistics.*

8 Cambridge University Press and Assessment, "Disagreement," Cambridge English Dictionary Online, accessed September 3, 2023, *https://dictionary.cambridge.org/us/dictionary/english/disagreement.*

9 Francesca Gino, "Disagreement Doesn't Have to Be Divisive," *Harvard Business Review*, November 16, 2020, *https://hbr.org/2020/11/disagreement-doesnt-have-to-be-divisive.*

CHAPTER 3

1 American Psychological Association, "Naïve Realism," APA Dictionary of Psychology, accessed September 11, 2023, *https://dictionary.apa.org/naive-realism.*

2 Sergio Mérida-López, Natalio Extremera, and Lourdes Rey, "Contributions of Work-Related Stress and Emotional Intelligence to Teacher Engagement: Additive and Interactive Effects," *International Journal of Environmental Research and Public Health* 14, no. 10 (2017): 1156, *https://doi.org/10.3390/ijerph14101156.*

CHAPTER 4

1 Sahar Andrade, MB.BCh., "Council Post: The Importance of Setting Healthy Boundaries," *Forbes*, November 9, 2022, *https://www.forbes.com/sites/forbescoachescouncil/2021/07/01/the-importance-of-setting-healthy-boundaries/?sh=195414856e46.*

2 Logan Hailey, "How to Set Boundaries: 5 Ways to Draw the Line Politely," Science of People, December 8, 2022, *https://www.scienceofpeople.com/how-to-set-boundaries/.*

CHAPTER 5

1 Robert Rosenthal and Lenore Jacobson, *Pygmalion in the Classroom: Teacher Expectation and Student Intellectual Development* (New York: Holt, Rinehart & Winston, 1968), 47.

2 David Tod, Emily J. Oliver, and James Hardy, "Effects of Self Talk: A Systematic Review," *Journal of Sport and Exercise Psychology* 33, no. 5 (2011): 666–87, *https://www.researchgate.net/publication/51704153_Effects_of_Self-Talk_A_Systematic_Review.*

3 Amy Morin, LCSW, "How Cognitive Reframing Works," Verywell Mind, May 10, 2023, *https://www.verywellmind.com/reframing-defined-2610419.*

4 Morin, "Cognitive Reframing."

5   Bruce D. Perry and Oprah Winfrey, *What Happened to You?: Conversations on Trauma, Resilience, and Healing* (New York: Flatiron, 2021).

6   Morin, "Cognitive Reframing."

7   "Selective Exposure Theory," Wikipedia, August 13, 2023, *https:// en.wikipedia.org/wiki/Selective_exposure_theory*.

8   Julia A. Minson, Frances S. Chen, and Catherine H. Tinsley, "Why Won't You Listen to Me? Measuring Receptiveness to Opposing Views," *Management Science* 66, no. 7 (2019): 3069–94, *https://doi .org/10.1287/mnsc.2019.3362*.

9   Michael Yeomans, Julia Minson, Hanne Collins, Frances Chen, and Francesca Gino, "Conversational Receptiveness: Improving Engagement with Opposing Views," *Organizational Behavior and Human Decision Processes* 160 (2020): 131–48, *https://doi.org /10.1016/j.obhdp.2020.03.011*.

10 Charles Dorison, Julia Minson, and Todd Rogers, "Selective Exposure Partly Relies on Faulty Affective Forecasts," *Cognition* 188 (2019): 98–107, *https://doi.org/10.1016/j.cognition.2019.02.010*.

11 William Hart, Dolores Albarracín, Alice H. Eagly, Inge Brechan, Matthew J. Lindberg, and Lisa Merrill, "Feeling Validated versus Being Correct: A Meta-analysis of Selective Exposure to Information," *Psychological Bulletin* 135, no. 4 (2009): 555–88, *https://doi .org/10.1037/a0015701*.

12 "Dehumanization," Dictionary.com, accessed September 2, 2023, *https://www.dictionary.com/browse/dehumanization*.

13 Juliana Schroeder, Michael Kardas, and Nicholas Epley, "The Humanizing Voice: Speech Reveals, and Text Conceals, a More Thoughtful Mind in the Midst of Disagreement," *Psychological Science* 28, no. 12 (2017): 1745–62, *https://doi.org/10.1177/0956797617713798*.

14 Nick Haslam and Steve Loughnan, "Dehumanization and Infrahumanization," *Annual Review of Psychology* 65 (2014): 399–423, *https://doi.org/10.1146/annurev-psych-010213-115045*.

15 Haslam and Loughnan, "Dehumanization and Infrahumanization."

16 Gordon Hodson and Kimberly Costello, "Interpersonal Disgust, Ideological Orientations, and Dehumanization as Predictors of

Intergroup Attitudes," *Psychological Science* 18, no. 8 (2007): 691–8, *https://doi.org/10.1111/j.1467-9280.2007.01962.x*

17 Kenneth D. Locke, "Aggression, Narcissism, Self-Esteem, and the Attribution of Desirable and Humanizing Traits to Self versus Others," *Journal of Research in Personality* 43, no. 1 (2009): 99–102, *https://doi.org/10.1016/j.jrp.2008.10.003*

18 Kurt Gray, Liane Young, and Adam Waytz, "Mind Perception Is the Essence of Morality," *Psychological Inquiry* 23, no. 2 (2012): 101–24, *https://doi.org/10.1080/1047840X.2012.651387.*

19 Kalina Christoff, "Dehumanization in Organizational Settings: Some Scientific and Ethical Considerations," *Frontiers in Human Neuroscience* 8 (2014): 748, *https://doi.org/10.3389/fnhum.2014.00748.*

20 "Humanize," Encyclopedia Britannica, accessed September 11, 2023, *https://www.britannica.com/dictionary/humanize.*

21 Emily Kubin, Kurt J. Gray, and Christian von Sikorski, "Reducing Political Dehumanization by Pairing Facts with Personal Experiences," *Political Psychology* 44, no. 5 (2023): 1119–40, *https://doi.org/10.1111/pops.12875.*

22 Christopher D. Petsko and Nour S. Kteily, "Political (Meta-) Dehumanization in Mental Representations: Divergent Emphases in the Minds of Liberals versus Conservatives," *Personality and Social Psychology Bulletin* (2023), *https://doi.org/10.1177/01461672231180971.*

23 American Psychological Association, "Inferiority Complex," APA Dictionary of Psychology, accessed September 11, 2023, *https://dictionary.apa.org/inferiority-complex?a=PGVV601G.*

24 Justin Jones-Fosu, *The Inclusive Mindset: How to Cultivate Diversity in Your Everyday Life* (Charlotte, NC: Peter Jones Publishing, 2021).

CHAPTER 6

1 Shane Barker, "How to Promote and Encourage a Learner's Mindset for Remote Teams," 360Learning, accessed September 11, 2023, *https://360learning.com/blog/learners-mindset/.*

2 Robert M. Yerkes and John D. Dodson, "The Relation of Strength of Stimulus to Rapidity of Habit-Formation," *Journal of Comparative Neurology* 18, no. 5 (1908): 459–82. *https://doi.org/10.1002/cne .920180503.*

3 Proverbs 18:15, *https://www.biblegateway.com/passage/?search =Proverbs%2018%3A15&version=ESV.*

4 Taya R. Cohen, Charles A. Dorison, Juliana Schroeder, Michael Yeomans, Xuan Zhao, Heather M. Caruso, Julia Alexandra Minson, and Jane Risen, "The Art and Science of Disagreeing: How to Create More Effective Conversations about Opposing Views," *Academy of Management Proceedings* 2020, no. 1 (2020): 15153, *https://doi.org /10.5465/ambpp.2020.15153symposium.*

5 Arbinger Institute, *The Anatomy of Peace: Resolving the Heart of Conflict*, 4th ed. (San Francisco: Berrett-Koehler, 2006).

6 Francesca Gino, "Disagreement Doesn't Have to Be Divisive," *Harvard Business Review*, November 16, 2020, *https://hbr.org/2020/11 /disagreement-doesnt-have-to-be-divisive.*

7 Justin Jones-Fosu, *The Inclusive Mindset: How to Cultivate Diversity in Your Everyday Life* (Charlotte, NC: Peter Jones Publishing, 2021).

8 Frances S. Chen, Julia A. Minson, and Zakary L. Tormala, "Tell Me More: The Effects of Expressed Interest on Receptiveness during Dialog," *Journal of Experimental Social Psychology* 46, no. 5 (2010): 850–53, *https://doi.org/10.1016/j.jesp.2010.04.012.*

9 Kenneth Savitsky, Boaz Keysar, Nicholas Epley, Travis Carter, and Ashley Swanson, "The Closeness-Communication Bias: Increased Egocentrism among Friends versus Strangers," *Journal of Experimental Social Psychology* 47, no. 1 (2011): 269–73, *https://doi.org /10.1016/j.jesp.2010.09.005.*

CHAPTER 7

1 University of Glasgow, "Remembering the Future: Our Brain Saves Energy by Predicting What It Will See," Medical Xpress, March 24, 2010, *https://medicalxpress.com/news/2010-03-future-brain-energy .html.*

2 Matthew Leonard, Maxime Baud, Matthias J. Sjerps, and Edward F. Change, "Perceptual Restoration of Masked Speech in Human Cortex," *Nature Communications* 7, no. 13619 (2016), *https://doi .org/10.1038/ncomms13619.*

3 Emily Pronin, Justin Kruger, Kenneth Savitsky, and Lee Ross, "You Don't Know Me, but I Know You: The Illusion of Asymmetric Insight," *Journal of Personality and Social Psychology* 81, no. 4 (2021): 639–56.

4 Taya R. Cohen, Charles A. Dorison, Juliana Schroeder, Michael Yeomans, Xuan Zhao, Heather M. Caruso, Julia Alexandra Minson, and Jane Risen, "The Art and Science of Disagreeing: How to Create More Effective Conversations about Opposing Views," *Academy of Management Proceedings* 2020, no. 1 (2020): 15153, *https://doi.org /10.5465/ambpp.2020.15153symposium.*

5 Jorge Faber and Lilian Martins Fonseca, "How Sample Size Influences Research Outcomes," *Dental Press Journal of Orthodontics* 19, no. 4 (2014): 27–29, *https://doi.org/10.1590/2176-9451.19.4.027-029.ebo.*

6 Chittaranjan Andrade, "Sample Size and its Importance in Research," *Indian Journal of Psychological Medicine* 42, no. 1 (2020): 102–3, *https://doi.org/10.4103/IJPSYM.IJPSYM_504_19.*

CHAPTER 8

1 Viola Lloyd, "Top Ten Benefits of Skilful Dialogue," theHRDIRECTOR, August 23, 2016, *https://www.thehrdirector.com/features/branding /top-ten-benefits-of-skilful-dialogue/.*

2 William Isaacs, *Dialogue and the Art of Thinking Together* (New York: Doubleday, 1999).

CHAPTER 9

1 Kathleen A. Kennedy and Emily Pronin, "When Disagreement Gets Ugly: Perceptions of Bias and the Escalation of Conflict," *Personality and Social Psychology Bulletin* 34, no. 6 (2008): 833–48, *https:// doi.org/10.1177/0146167208315158.*

2 Justine Zhang, Jonathan Chang, Cristian Danescu-Niculescu-Mizil, Lucas Dixon, Yiqing Hua, Dario Taraborelli, and Nithum Thain, "Conversations Gone Awry: Detecting Early Signs of Conversational Failure," in *Proceedings of the 56th Annual Meeting of the Association for Computational Linguistics (Volume 1: Long Papers)*, ed. Iryna Gurevych and Yusuke Miyao (Melbourne: Association for Computational Linguistics, 2018), *https://doi.org/10.18653/v1/p18-1125*.

3 Juliana Schroeder, Michael Kardas, and Nicholas Epley, "The Humanizing Voice: Speech Reveals, and Text Conceals, a More Thoughtful Mind in the Midst of Disagreement," *Psychological Science* 28, no. 12 (2017): 1745–62, *https://doi.org/10.1177/0956797617713798*.

4 Michael Yeomans, Julia Minson, Hanne Collins, Frances Chen, and Francesca Gino, "Conversational Receptiveness: Improving Engagement with Opposing Views," *Organizational Behavior and Human Decision Processes* 160 (2020): 131–48, *https://doi.org/10.1016/j.obhdp.2020.03.011*.

5 Francesca Gino, "Disagreement Doesn't Have to Be Divisive," *Harvard Business Review*, November 16, 2020, *https://hbr.org/2020/11/disagreement-doesnt-have-to-be-divisive*.

6 Yeomans et al., "Conversational Receptiveness."

7 Taya R. Cohen, Charles A. Dorison, Juliana Schroeder, Michael Yeomans, Xuan Zhao, Heather M. Caruso, Julia Alexandra Minson, and Jane Risen, "The Art and Science of Disagreeing: How to Create More Effective Conversations about Opposing Views," *Academy of Management Proceedings* 2020, no. 1 (2020): 15153, *https://doi.org/10.5465/ambpp.2020.15153symposium*.

8 Jane McGuire, "Runner Sacrifices His Own Race to Help Exhausted Runner across the Line," *Runner's World*, September 12, 2019, *https://www.runnersworld.com/uk/news/a29018927/runner-help-exhausted-runner-across-the-line/*.

9 Schroeder et al., "The Humanizing Voice."

10 John A. Bargh and Katelyn Y. McKenna, "The Internet and Social Life," *Annual Review of Psychology* 55, no. 1 (2004): 573–90, *https://doi.org/10.1146/annurev.psych.55.090902.141922*.

11 Schroeder et al., "The Humanizing Voice."

CHAPTER 10

1 Andrea Trudslev and Oliver Gustavsen, "Unjudge Someone," Human Library Organization, May 9, 2023, *https://humanlibrary.org/*.

RESOURCES

1 Marily Oppezzo and Daniel L. Schwartz, "Give Your Ideas Some Legs: The Positive Effect of Walking on Creative Thinking," *Journal of Experimental Psychology: Learning, Memory, and Cognition* 40, no. 4 (2014): 1142–52, *https://doi.org/10.1037/a0036577*.

RESOURCES

I n this section you will find a series of 10 Quick Tips from Work. Meaningful. for individuals, leaders, and those navigating the political divide. Please also visit the Resources section of *HowToRespectfullyDisagree.com* for the following:

- Ways we have worked with clients to create a customized approach to creating Golden Respect in the workplace

- Information on our I Respectfully Disagree course, a fun micro-learning and self-paced course to help you build your respectful disagreement muscles (and plus you get to see me . . . ha!)

- My TEDx title: "Don't Take the Exit On People," which is eighteen minutes of pure fun and reflection

- Recommended books, articles, and videos to help you dive deeper

- Practical ways to help your organization and communities live out these values

- Other valuable resources to help you bridge the divide in your everyday life

If you feel your organization may benefit from our work, visit us at *WorkMeaningful.com* or email us at *engage @workmeaningful.com*.

RESOURCE 1: 10 QUICK TIPS TO HELP INDIVIDUALS RESPECTFULLY DISAGREE

For a more detailed tip guide and updated information, please visit *HowToRespectfullyDisagree.com* and go to the Resources section. We are constantly updating this information with relevant resources and tools to apply this guidance to our everyday lives.

1. ALWAYS MAINTAIN AN OPEN HEART, WHETHER YOU HAVE AN OPEN OR CLOSED MIND.

Embrace empathy. Even if you can't change your mind, you can always empathize and understand where the other person is coming from. Holding compassion and care in conversations allows for more fruitful exchanges.

2. DO A SELF-AWARENESS CHECK-IN.

Check your mental and emotional state. Are you in a position to have a constructive conversation? If you're already feeling stressed or overwhelmed, it might be best to delay the conversation until you're better equipped emotionally and mentally.

Check your physical well-being. Fatigue and hunger can influence your mood. Ensure you're physically ready to engage in disagreement.

3. ADOPT A LEARNER'S MINDSET.

Gather resources. Books, seminars, and workshops that focus on effective communication or understanding different perspectives can be valuable.

Ask questions over making statements. Instead of making a statement, ask questions to understand the root of the other person's belief or perspective.

4. ALWAYS ACKNOWLEDGE.

Use the 3FA Model. The 3FA Model is simply about acknowledging a person and appreciating them for sharing their perspective. You can fully acknowledge someone whether you (1) completely disagree, (2) partially agree, or (3) fully agree. The point is that full acknowledgment is always possible.

Use "Thank you, because." Always follow up with a "Thank you, because." Showing appreciation for their perspective and detailing why it's valuable helps foster respect.

5. TAKE THE CIRCLES OF GRACE CHALLENGE.

Repeat the challenge regularly. Every six months, engage in beliefs or with people that you disagree with to identify places of learning and understanding. Go to events, participate in experiences, and talk to people who hold such views.

Engage without judgment. Try discussing with a neutral stance, seeking understanding above all.

6. EMBRACE THE POWER OF DEEP LISTENING.

Actively listen. Apply the Power of 3 by repeating or paraphrasing what the person said, asking clarifying questions, and then responding.

Encourage elaboration. Using phrases like "Tell me more" gives them space to expand on their thoughts, making them feel heard and valued.

7. CULTIVATE THE 5 PILLARS OF BRIDGING THE DIVIDE.

Choose one. Select one pillar and draft a plan to enhance this skill over the next ninety days.

8. SEEK THE GRAY AREA.

Look beyond black and white. Life is seldom binary. Asking yourself "Where is the gray?" can help you identify common ground or nuances in disagreements.

9. TAKE THE NO DISAGREEMENT CHALLENGE.

Practice restraint for twenty-four hours. This doesn't mean suppressing your views, but rather not actively opposing someone else's. It's a practice in restraint and deep listening. Remember, it's just for twenty-four hours!

10. PRACTICE COGNITIVE REFRAMING.

Analyze your self-talk. How you talk to yourself about disagreements can shape their outcome. Positive self-talk and reframing how you view the disagreement can pave the way for more respectful interactions.

Reflect on your belief systems about yourself and others. Sometimes disagreements stem more from our personal insecurities and biases than from actual issues.

The essence of respectful disagreement is rooted in understanding, patience, and the genuine desire to communicate. While disagreements are natural, they can be a gateway to deeper understanding and growth if approached with the right mindset.

RESOURCE 2: 10 QUICK TIPS TO HELP LEADERS BRIDGE THE DIVIDE

For a more detailed tip guide and updated information, please visit *HowToRespectfullyDisagree.com* and go to the Resources section. We are constantly updating this information with relevant resources and tools to apply this guidance to our everyday lives.

1. MODEL THE BEHAVIOR.

Lead by example. Regularly demonstrate how to handle disagreements with respect, showcasing active listening and seeking understanding over confrontation.

Engage in feedback loops. Regularly solicit feedback on your behavior, demonstrating that you're open to reflection and growth.

2. EXPRESS VULNERABILITY.

Share personal growth stories. Openly discuss past conflicts, highlighting the growth and understanding that resulted from them.

Hold open forums. Host sessions where team members can share personal stories of growth from conflict, emphasizing learning over blame.

3. REWARD DISAGREEMENT.

Promote diverse voices. Make it clear that all voices, regardless of hierarchy, have value and are encouraged to speak up.

Implement recognition systems. Introduce awards or incentives for team members who exemplify constructive disagreement.

4. CULTIVATE A LEARNING CULTURE.

Hold regular learning sessions. Schedule monthly or quarterly sessions dedicated to enhancing communication skills.

Promote peer learning. Encourage team members to share insights from courses or books that foster understanding and healthy debate.

5. SEEK OPPOSING PERSPECTIVES.
Set aside time in meeting agendas for other opinions. Include a segment dedicated to exploring alternate viewpoints on key issues.

Assign rotational roles. Have team members take turns in different roles to represent contrasting viewpoints, ensuring a spectrum of perspectives.

6. ENCOURAGE THE CIRCLES OF GRACE CHALLENGE.
Lead a challenge. Create an opportunity for your team/employees to learn about people or groups they disagree with over three to six months. They can attend events, read about their ideas, and talk to people directly in the groups. They should ask what they learned about the group/ideas and what they learned about themselves as they experienced it. Let us know if you need assistance.

Explain the guidelines. Provide clear guidance on what the Circle of Grace Challenge entails—listening actively, avoiding blame, and seeking clarity. This is not an opportunity to share why you disagree but rather to better understand other perspectives!

7. GROW YOUR GRATITUDE.
Implement daily gratitude practices. Encourage team members to start their day by acknowledging something they're grateful for.

Use shared platforms to express thanks. Use tools or boards where team members can pin appreciation notes for one another.

8. LEAD RESPECTFUL MEETINGS.
Establish the ground rules. Begin every meeting by setting (or reminding attendees of) ground rules.

Give equal time. Use tools or techniques like a speaking stick to ensure everyone gets a fair chance to voice their opinions.

9. SEEK THE GRAY AND INNOVATE FROM FRICTION.
Hold brainstorming sessions. Use disagreements as a launching pad for brainstorming sessions. This will show that diverse views yield unique and innovative solutions.

Pause for post-conflict reflection. After disagreements, dedicate time to extract learning points and potential areas of innovation that surfaced.

10. HOLD WALKING MEETINGS FOR TOUGH TOPICS.
Designate certain routes. Identify specific, tranquil routes conducive for in-depth conversations. Research has shown that walking meetings can enhance innovation and team cohesiveness.[1]

Switch up pairings. Rotate walking partners regularly to ensure everyone gets the opportunity to engage with different perspectives.

The underlying principle in fostering an environment of respectful disagreement is to move from a mindset of confrontation to one of collaboration. When leaders create spaces where differences are not just tolerated but celebrated, they lay the foundation for a more innovative, understanding, and cohesive team.

RESOURCE 3: 10 QUICK TIPS FOR ANYONE NAVIGATING THE POLITICAL DIVIDE

For a more detailed tip guide and updated information, please visit *HowToRespectfullyDisagree.com* and go to the Resources section. We are constantly updating this information with relevant resources and tools to apply this guidance to our everyday lives.

1. CHOOSE HOPE OVER HATE.

Reframe your perspective. Understand that hope is a choice. By constantly expecting the worst in others, you create barriers before a conversation even begins.

Open your heart. While you might have non-negotiable beliefs, it's crucial to keep an open heart. Recognizing the humanity in those with differing political views is the first step in bridging the gap.

2. FIND GROUPS WHERE YOU CAN HAVE CONSISTENT DIALOGUE.

Join existing groups. Platforms like the Human Library or Living Room Conversations offer safe environments to engage with diverse perspectives.

Remember that consistency is key. One-off encounters rarely lead to substantial change. Commit to regular interactions for deeper understanding.

3. PRACTICE ACTIVE LISTENING WITH LOVED ONES.

Set intentions. Before starting, let them know you're in a listening mode. Your goal is understanding, not debate.

Ask open-ended questions. This encourages them to share more deeply and thoughtfully.

4. SEEK THE GRAY.

Focus on shared interests first. Begin by discussing mutual interests or values. This establishes trust and rapport.

Navigate the nuances. Recognize that most issues aren't black and white. Delve into the nuances together.

5. OPT FOR MEANINGFUL CONVERSATION PLATFORMS.

Avoid impersonal platforms. Social media often promotes shallow, combative exchanges.

Prioritize personal interaction. Calls, in-person meet-ups, or video chats allow for deeper, more genuine conversations.

6. STOP THINKING AND START TALKING.

Break down assumptions. Recognize that assumptions about others' beliefs can be wrong. Don't let these beliefs dictate how you treat them.

Seek first-hand knowledge. Conversing directly with someone offers more authentic insights than assumptions.

7. WALK AND TALK.

Combine physical activity and dialogue. Walking side by side can ease tension and foster better conversation.

Engage in a shared experience. As with walking, doing any activity together can act as a buffer during challenging discussions.

8. CELEBRATE INDIVIDUALITY.

Question party dogma. It's okay to not align 100 percent with every stance your preferred political party takes.

Engage in self-reflection. Regularly evaluate your beliefs. It's okay for them to evolve based on new information or experiences.

9. TRUST BUT VERIFY.

Cross-check facts. Ensure your information comes from credible, varied sources.

Promote fact-based discussions. Encourage others to do their own research, and approach discussions with a focus on understanding.

10. RECOGNIZE THE UGLY TRUTH.

Avoid the power play. Understand that for many people, politics is a game of power, ratings, and optics. With that knowledge, filter how you approach topics for better understanding rather than the loudest voices.

Seek genuine engagement. Instead of being swayed by the noise, seek genuine, heart-to-heart engagements.

Remember, bridging the political divide is not about converting or convincing, but about understanding and coexisting. Mutual respect and patience are pivotal in these efforts.

RESOURCE 4: DISCUSSION GUIDE

Engaging with *I Respectfully Disagree* has hopefully illuminated the nuanced art of valuing each individual's inherent worth, even amidst differing perspectives. The goal was to spark fresh inquiries, revelations, and an eagerness to delve further into these themes, both in your professional and personal spheres.

Use the "Reflections and Actions" sections at the end of each chapter to answer for yourself or your team how to incorporate the chapter's guidance into your everyday lives.

For a more in-depth and detailed Discussion Guide, please visit *HowToRespectfullyDisagree.com* and go to the Resources section. We are constantly updating this information with relevant resources and tools for individuals, teams, and organizations.

RESOURCE 5: A RECAP OF THE 5 PILLARS

Congratulations on engaging the 5 Pillars of Bridging the Divide as your foundation for personal and professional growth and development. Each pillar represents a key aspect of personal transformation, and by incorporating it into your daily routine, you can unlock new opportunities and foster a mindset of continuous learning and growth.

PILLAR 1: CHALLENGE YOUR PERSPECTIVE
To challenge your perspective, you must actively seek out alternative viewpoints and question your own assumptions. Here are some actions you can take to implement this pillar:

- **Seek diverse perspectives.** Surround yourself with individuals from different backgrounds, cultures, and beliefs. Actively engage in discussions and events that challenge your worldview and expose you to new ideas. Choose to give value to every human being regardless of stance, status, or background.

- **Read broadly.** Explore literature, articles, and books from various genres, authors, and perspectives. Delve into subjects you are unfamiliar with to broaden your knowledge and understanding.

PILLAR 2: BE THE STUDENT

Embracing your inner student means adopting a mindset of constant learning and personal growth. Here are some strategies to help you embody this pillar:

- **Set learning goals.** Identify specific areas of interest or skills you would like to develop. Set achievable goals and create a plan to acquire new knowledge or enhance your existing abilities.

- **Seek feedback.** Actively seek feedback from mentors, peers, or experts in the field you wish to grow in. Be open to constructive criticism and use it as an opportunity for improvement.

- **Reflect on experiences.** Take time to reflect on your experiences and identify lessons learned. Analyze both successes and failures to extract valuable insights that will contribute to your personal and professional development.

PILLAR 3: CULTIVATE YOUR CURIOSITY

Cultivating curiosity involves nurturing an inquisitive mindset and a desire to explore the unknown by asking meaningful questions. Here's how you can embrace this pillar:

- **Ask questions.** Instead of accepting things at face value, ask questions to deepen your understanding. Challenge assumptions and explore the underlying reasons behind what you encounter.

- **Experiment and explore.** Step out of your comfort zone and try new activities, hobbies, or experiences. Engaging in unfamiliar endeavors can spark creativity and expand your horizons.

- **Stay open-minded and open-hearted.** Embrace uncertainty and be willing to consider alternative perspectives. Approach new ideas or information with a sense of curiosity and a willingness to learn.

PILLAR 4: SEEK THE GRAY

Seeking the gray is about embracing complexity and recognizing that the world is not always black and white. Here's how you can practice this pillar:

- **Seek nuance.** Avoid simplistic binary thinking and strive to understand the intricacies of any given situation. Consider multiple factors and perspectives before forming judgments or making decisions.

- **Embrace ambiguity.** Be comfortable with uncertainty and learn to navigate situations where clearcut answers may not exist. Practice patience and allow space for ambiguity in your decision-making process.

PILLAR 5: AGREE TO RESPECT

Respect is essential in fostering positive relationships and creating a harmonious environment. Here's how you can incorporate this pillar into your life:

- **Fully acknowledge others.** Acknowledge those you disagree with and thank them for sharing their view, even if it differs from your own. Treat everyone with kindness, empathy, and respect.

- **Embrace difference and inclusion.** Value and appreciate the uniqueness of individuals from different backgrounds, cultures, and beliefs. Create an inclusive environment by first asking what it looks like for each person when they feel respected and valued.

By incorporating these actions into your daily life, you will not only deepen your understanding of the 5 Pillars but also create a solid foundation for personal growth and development. Remember that transformation is a continuous process, and by embracing these pillars, you will be embarking on a lifelong journey of self-improvement and fulfillment.

Let's make this world a little better by respecting the people in it a lot more!

ACKNOWLEDGMENTS

I first want to thank my mother (mom-e) for your intentionality in making sure that I not only experienced difference but always engaged things we disagreed with. You were building up my respectful disagreement muscles and I had no idea. I would not be in a position to write this book without your wonderful child rearing (but no more washing dishes for me . . . ha!).

Thank you to Tanya, Isaiah, Lydia, Peter, and David for being the best family in the whole world. You make me a better husband and dad-e and you have taught me so much about being respectful in disagreements. Thank you for challenging my ego and helping me ask more questions.

Thank you to my Work. Meaningful. team who allowed me to focus on this project while you all carried the workload (often without me). Dari, you are a rock star, and we would not have the business we have today without you! To our Ghana team . . . *medaase* . . . this process has been an amazing journey, and I am grateful for all the hard work and effort you put into the business on my many writing retreats.

Thank you to my Mastermind Group: Stan, Marcey, Kevin, Cynthia, and Raven (miss you, Jeff). Your constant encouragement has kept me going and your continual challenges have kept me growing! I love our monthly meetings and our MANY inside jokes. I look forward to seeing you all on the big stage!

Steve Piersanti—my kindred brother. I could not have asked for a better editor. You believed in this project when I didn't believe in myself. You gave me hope when I had many doubts. I am so grateful we connected and were able to build this together. Let me know if you add more rules to your basketball squad because they are ingenious! Thank you to Jennifer Kahnweiler for connecting us and encouraging me to connect with BK!

A special thank you to my mentors along the way. Susan Johnson, you continue to inspire me with your heart, wit, brilliance, and special ability to convey tough topics with grace! Forest Harper, I always love our impromptu calls and texts where you challenge me to go further than I thought I could go. Babs Smith and Dan Sullivan, you have helped my business grow and scale and given me a view of what Work. Meaningful. can really be.

To the Work. Meaningful. Foundation board members, thank you for believing in the vision to make this world a little more meaningful and for all you are doing to help improve education on the continent of Africa and in the United States. Can you believe that we are almost done building our first school?!

To my AWESOME clients, from the Fortune 50 all the way to the Fortunate Fourth Graders! It has been such a pleasure serving you all these years, and our countless learning experiences gave birth to this book. While I shared with you, I was learning at the same time.

Thank you to all those who took time to interview with me officially and unofficially. Hassan, the work you are doing continues to be a beacon of light in a sometimes-dim world. Keep the conversation going. Matt, thank you for our many disagreements in person and over the phone. I haven't always respectfully disagreed, and I appreciate the grace you have given me along the journey. Because I changed your names in the book, I cannot thank you directly, but you know who you are and I am thankful!

Thank you to those who helped me, challenged me, and gave me space to write and create. Lydia and Peter, you held it down while dad-e had to pull all-nighters to get this book done, and I owe you some much-needed quality time! Are you ready for Nerf Wars . . . lol! Thank you to Jon Clemons, Darryl Bellamy, and the entire Berrett-Koehler publishing team. You have made this process so much easier for me. To my advance readers . . . wow! Your feedback was tough but fair, and while there were some points I respectfully disagreed with you on, ultimately you made the book much better by addressing my many blind spots.

Last but not least, thank YOU for investing in this book and reading it. I hope we continue to create an amazing world for today and tomorrow by adding A LOT more humanity to it!

INDEX

A

A Time to Kill, 99–100
abuse
    inferiority complex from, 105
    and mistreatment of others,
      162
    moving away from, 103
    physical, 54–55
accuracy, 140
acknowledgment
    in 3FA model, 170–172, 199
    as a choice, 168
    of disagreement, 201
    to reduce divisiveness, 166
    as respect, 178, 209
action/activism
    Heart. Head. Hand. Model
      for, 9
    of Nelson Mandela, 68
    respectful, 47–48
    small, consistent, 183
advice, unsolicited, 33–35
aggressiveness, passive, 29, 42
agreeing to disagree, 3, 50, 170
agreement
    in 3FA model, 170–172
    facade of, 29, 42
    highlighting, 167
    respect as, 71
alcohol, 165
ambiguity, 158, 209
apartheid, 67–68
apologies, 185–186

arguments, 123
assumptions
    breaking down, 205
    emotional force of, 166
    as inevitable, 138
    and knowledge gaps, 132
    questions rather than, 134
    as "taking the exit," 129
asymmetric insight, illusion of,
    135–136
awareness of self, 198

B

balance
    boundaries and, 74
    of debate and discovery, 154
    of Equal Self, 108
    between honesty and
      conflict, 26
    how to maintain, 108
    of humility and confidence,
      118–119
    of power, 40
    of self, 108
barriers
    vs. boundaries, 76
    bridges vs., 69, 186
    confirmation bias as, 97
    disagreements as, 29
    kindness to dismantle, 163
behavior change, 201
beliefs
    adjusting, 120

beliefs *(continued)*
    illusion of asymmetric insight, 135–136
    low-/high-commitment, 98, 166
    reality as defined by, 88, 90
    reflecting on your, 200
bias
    commitment to, 161–162
    confirmation bias, 95–97
    confronting your, 107
    learning, 59
    transformation of, 161–163
blanks, filling in
    conscious effort to avoid, 136
    dangers of assumption, 133–135
    familiarity and, 125–126
    via perceptual restoration, 133
body language, 170
Boipatong massacre, 68
books, recommended, 197
boundaries
    case study of, 77–78
    how to set, 77, 79–80
    patience of, 80–82
    for respectful disagreement, 74–77
Bourdain, Anthony, 15
breaks, taking, 79
bridges, building
    via 3FA model, 170
    alternative to, 29
    via apology, 186
    author's experience of, 7
    barriers vs., 69
    via constructive dialogue, 122–123
    disagreement as chance for, 12
    via kindness, 163
    leadership in, 200–204
    need for, 83
    by Nelson Mandela, 68
    See also 5 Pillars of Bridging the Divide

C
cathartic release, 176
challenges
    Circle of Grace Challenge, 146, 183, 199, 202
    confidence for, 119
    to our perspectives, 99–100
    in personal history, 57–58
    reshaping narrative on, 91–92
    of respectful disagreement, 28
    rising to, 10, 21
    to your perspective, 70
change
    via compassion, 163–164
    via empathy, 73
    means to create, 43
    modeling, 201
    planting seeds of, 50
    starting with small, 60
Chinese culture, 168–170
choice
    to bridge the divide, 73–74
    in each moment, 186
    forgiveness as a, 55
    as human freedom/right, 47
    power of, 89–91
    reality as defined by, 90–91
    respect as a, 46, 48–49
circle of grace
    defined, 95
    expanding our, 131, 132
    separating person/views outside, 164
Circle of Grace Challenge, 146, 183, 199, 202
coercive power, 39
cognitive reframing, 89, 91–93, 200
collaboration, 148–149, 166, 169, 173
comfort zone, leaving, 141
common ground, 69, 145, 167, 170, 173

communication
    mediums for, 174–176, 205
    modes of, 164
    open, 79
compassion
    holding, 198
    for ourselves, 91–92
    retaliation vs., 48
    transformation via, 163
competition, 147–148, 171
complexity, 141, 146
comprehension, 123–126
compromise, 68, 149
conditioning
    via family pattern, 58
    via pivotal life moments, 57
confidence, 118–119
conflict
    conversational, 164
    four responses to, 27–28
    global statistics, 2–3
    habituation toward, 162
    listening to defuse, 4
    reflection following, 203
    unaddressed, 22
    understanding amidst, 68, 69
confrontation
    fear of, 22–23
    habituation toward, 162
    tools to avoid, 167
congeniality bias, 95–97
consent, 177
constructive dialogue, 76, 113–115,
    122–123
conversation
    avoiding difficult, 22–23
    out of control, 164
    three levels of listening in, 122
    timing of, 62, 63, 165
conversational receptiveness
    and culture, 168–170
    lack of, 164
    and newness, 109–110
    recipe for, 166–167
    in the workplace, 4

counseling, 35
courage
    compassion as, 48
    curiosity as, 137–138
    in Golden Respect, 39
    to share alternate perspective,
        173
courtesy, 172
culture
    of learning, 201
    polarized, 1–2
    and receptiveness, 168–170
    respect and, 41–42
curiosity
    in the 5 Pillars of Bridging,
        71, 208
    vs. acceptance, 134
    vs. anger, 166
    as courageous, 137–138
    cultivating, 208
    debate vs. discovery, 151–152
    Dotted Line Dilemma,
        133–135
    joy of, 137
    vs. jumping to conclusions,
        132–133
    vs. small sample size,
        138–141
    vs. taking the exit, 131–132
    as "tell me more," 134
Curious George, 136–137

D
debates, 151–154
decision-making, 40
dehumanization
    as a barrier, 69–70
    via bias, 59
    choice in the face of, 47
    defined, 100
    factors increasing, 101–102
    and humanization, 103–104
    race and, 99–100
    respectful dissent vs., 3
    superiority and, 106

demeanor, 170
dialogue
    constructive, 76, 113–115
    embracing meaningful, 97
    on political matters, 204
    power of, 155–157
    respectful, 50
    terms for, 172
Dialogue: The Art of Thinking Together, 156
differences
    embracing, 96, 97, 209
    with high-commitment beliefs, 98
    respectful response to, 50
    understanding of, 124
    violence resulting from, 2–3
dignity, 155
diplomacy, 68
"Disagreement Doesn't Have to Be Divisive," 166
disagreement(s)
    avoiding, 184
    as barriers, 29
    benefit of, 151
    on big and small topics, 13
    big impacts from small, 21
    boundaries in, 74–77, 80
    bridging, 69
    as competition, 147–148
    constructive, 113–115
    defined, 49–50
    effect of power on, 39–41
    and fight mode, 56
    four responses to, 28
    gray area in, 151
    guilty pleasure in, 49–50, 123
    humanizing, 7, 103, 177–178, 182
    intentional exposure to, 199
    learned patterns in, 57, 58
    made personal, 164
    naïve realism in, 60–62
    No Disagreement Challenge, 184, 200
    non-divisive, 166–167
    as opportunity, 12
    patience for, 80
    pervasiveness of, 25
    positive self-talk about, 89
    questions amidst, 137
    rewarding, 201
    taking a break from, 62
    viewed as disrespect, 43–45
discoveries, 151–152
Discussion Guide, 206–207
dishonesty, 22
disrespect
    in agreeing to disagree, 170
    disagreement as presumed, 43–45
    guilty pleasure in, 123
    moving to respect from, 29–30
    polarized, 2
    respect in the face of, 48
    verbal attacks as, 43
disrespectful agreement, 16, 17, 28, 30, 46, 105, 182, 184
disrespectful disagreement, 16, 28, 30, 184
diversity
    intentionally embracing, 111, 178
    savoring, 124
    vs. small sample size, 138–141
divisions of opinion
    honoring, 11
    intentional exposure to, 6
    polarization and, 1–2
"Don't Take the Exit On People," 197
Dotted Line Dilemma, 133–135

E

education, 198
emails, 175
emotional health
    and engaging disagreements, 165

and safety, 75, 80–81
self check-ins for, 198
taking breaks for, 79
and timing of dialogue, 62, 63
empathy
change via, 73
cognitive reframing and,
91–92, 94, 104
comprehension for, 125
embracing, 198
humanization via, 103
as a mirror, 163
need for, 4
with our in-group, 164
Equal Self, 108–109
errors, 185–186
escalation prevention, 76
expectations, 90
expert power, 39

F

FA+FA (Full Acknowledgment,
Full Agreement), 171
FA+NA (Full Acknowledgment,
No Agreement), 171
FA+PA (Full Acknowledgment,
Partial Agreement), 171
face-to-face communication, 175
familiarity, 125–126
family
active listening with, 204
boundaries with, 75
healing within, 129–130
navigating issues in, 4
patterns in/taken from, 58–60
"superiority" of parents,
106–107
treating all as, 12
feedback, 126, 201, 208
fitting in, 6
5 Pillars of Bridging the Divide
applying, 184–185
cultivating, 199
as foundational, 14
by leadership, 200–204

overview of, 29, 70–71, 85,
207–210
Pillar 1, 87–111, 207
Pillar 2, 113–127, 208
Pillar 3, 129–142, 208–209
Pillar 4, 145–158, 209
Pillar 5, 161–179, 209–210
potential bridges/barriers in,
16, 71–72
fly-on-the-wall principle, 117
forgiveness
as a choice, 55
power of, 56
Four Responses of Conversation
Conflict, 16–17
Frankl, Victor, 47
Franklin, Aretha, 35–36
freedom, 47, 48
Full Acknowledgment (FA), 171

G

generative listening, 156
Ghiassi, Hassan, 121, 137
Golden Respect
10 characteristics of, 37–38
applying, 184
barriers to, 16
as a choice, 33
defined, 11
as a gift, 39
heart work to reach, 53, 56
resources, 197
Golden Rule, 155, 174
gratitude, 166, 202
gray area
in the 5 Pillars of Bridging,
71, 209
via collaboration, 148–149
in dialogue, 155–157
as discovery, 152–154
learning to see, 145–147
life examples of, 149–151
seeking the, 200, 203, 205, 209
growth, personal
in 3Self model, 108–109

growth *(continued)*
    confronting biases for, 107
    via dialogue, 156
    Heart. Head. Hand. Model, 9
    ripple effects of, 10
    willingness to allow, 26–27

H

harmony, false, 28
Harvard Business Review, 166
hate, 161–162, 204
healing, 129–130
heard, feeling, 5, 173
heart, open, 198, 209
Heart. Head. Hand. Model, 9
"hedging your claims," 167, 184
helplessness, 40
high-commitment beliefs, 98, 166
history, personal
    author's, 53–56
    effects of, 16
    and inferiority complex, 105
    and mistreatment of
        others, 162
    pivotal moments in, 57–58
hope, 204
HowToRespectfullyDisagree.com,
    197, 198, 200, 204
Human Library, 181–182
humanity/humanization
    as a bridge, 69–70
    change via shared, 73
    as a choice, 47
    competition or, 173
    defined, 102–103
    dehumanization and, 103–104
    via dialogue, 156
    factors increasing, 102–103
    via giving of self, 49
    learning via, 11
    respect as honoring, 46–48
    universal acknowledgment
        of, 7
    verbal mediums for, 174–176
    via voice, 164

humility, 118–119, 165
Hutchinson, Patrick, 48–49

I

"I hear that, and," 172
I Respectfully Disagree course, 197
"I" statements, 79, 167
illusion of asymmetric insight,
    135–136
inclusion, 178
Inclusive Mindset
    defined, 7
    vision of the, 8
    workshops, 11
The Inclusive Mindset: How to
    Cultivate Diversity in Your
    Everyday Life, 7, 107, 122
inclusivity, 7, 209
individuality, 89–90, 205
inequality, challenging, 43, 47–48
Inferior Self, 105–106, 108
inferiority complex, 105
in-group/out-group
    assumptions and, 132
    behavior interpretations of, 95
    as "circle of grace," 95, 131,
        146, 164
    dehumanization and, 101
    empathy and, 164
    upbringing as shaping our, 59
inquiry, 157
insights, shared, 183
inverted U concept, 118–119
Isaacs, William, 156–157

J

journaling, 92, 184
judgments of others, 93, 157

K

kindness, 163

L

leadership
    bridge building by, 200–204

respectful dissent allowed by, 41
without dissent, 43–45
learner's mindset, 115–116, 198
learning
in the 5 Pillars of Bridging, 70, 208
as available everywhere, 119–121
via collaboration, 148–149
via comprehension, 125
via constructive dialogue, 113–115
culture of, 201
goals for, 126, 208
Heart. Head. Hand. Model for, 9
via humanization, 11
impediments to, 118
intelligence as openness to, 119
learner's mindset, 115–116, 198, 208
via listening, 116–117, 121–123, 170
from mistakes, 120
optimal space for, 118–119
seeking out, 199
legitimate power, 39
Leonard, Matthew, 132
Life Disagreement Markers (LDMs), 57–58
listening
deeply, 199, 204
in diplomacy, 68
in the face of hate, 162
generative, 156
harmony via, 4
vs. illusion of asymmetric insight, 135–136
importance of, 120
learning and, 116, 121–123, 170
in new circumstances, 125–126

planting seeds via, 50
to spoken word, 175
three levels of, 122

M
Mandela, Nelson, 67–68, 83
margin of error, 140
mediation, 80
meetings, 203
mental health, 62, 63, 165, 198
mindful sharing, 177–178
miscommunication, 125
mistakes, 185–186
misunderstanding, 134, 174

N
naïve realism, 60–62
narcissism, 101–102
narratives, reframing, 91–92, 95
negative thoughts, 91–92
newness
avoiding, 131–132
negative newness, 110
openness to, 142
and over-enthusiasm, 120–121
patience in learning, 124
sharing, 183
"No, because," 172
No Disagreement Challenge, 184, 200
nonconfrontation, 167
"norm," the, 140
nuance, 151, 158, 209

O
objectivity, 60–62
online forums, 174, 175
open forums, 201
openness, 142, 162, 198, 209
opinions
adjusting, 120
outlying, 140
people as separate from, 164

"other"
  in 5 Pillars model, 85
  cognitive reframing and,
    93–95
  and congeniality bias, 97
  dehumanization of, 103–104
  hearing the voice of, 174
  humanizing the, 73, 87
  mistrust of, 162
  seeing the, 69
outlying opinions, 140
outspoken, being, 46

P

participation, 157
passive aggressiveness, 29, 42
past, personal. *See* history,
  personal
patience
  boundaries and, 80–82
  comprehension via, 124
  and conversational
    receptiveness, 109
  in the face of hate, 163
peace, 138
peer learning, 202
perceptual restoration, 132
perfection, 28, 60
permission, asking, 177
personality
  disorders, and
    dehumanization, 101–102
  respect and, 46
perspective(s)
  broadening your, 26–27,
    111, 155
  challenging your, 70, 99–100,
    207
  as a choice, 89–91
  considering alternate,
    122, 166
  familiarity via, 95–96
  and illusion of asymmetric
    insight, 135–136
  of an inferiority complex, 106

learner's mindset, 115–116
naïve realism about your,
  60–62
openness to new, 129–130
as personal choice, 47
reality as defined by,
  87–89, 90
receptive, 170
rejecting others', 173
seed planting to change, 50
seeking alternate, 202, 207
sharing, 152, 165, 176–178
shifts, 11
understanding others', 59–60
persuasiveness, 121, 164, 167
Pew Research Center, 2
phone communication, 175
physical abuse, 54–55
physical state, 165, 198
politeness, 42–43
political disagreement
  boundaries about, 75
  and congeniality bias, 97
  between family members,
    23–24
  gray area in, 145–146
  Nelson Mandela's response
    to, 67–68
  tips for navigating, 204–206
power
  absolute workplace authority,
    43–45
  to bridge the divide, 74
  of conversational
    receptiveness, 167
  and dehumanization, 102
  of dialogue, 155–157
  effect on disagreement,
    39–41
  of expectations, 87–88
  of forgiveness, 55
  play, political, 206
  sharing, 56
Power of 3, 122, 184
problem-solving, 125, 155

protesting inequality, 43
psychopathy, 101–102

Q

QS Method, 177–178
questions, asking, 137, 141,
    177–178, 184, 198, 208

R

racism, 99–100, 161
reaction, 166
reading broadly, 207
realism, naïve, 60–62
receptiveness, conversational, 4,
    109–110
Redding, Otis, 36
redemption, 161, 163
referent power, 39
reframing
    cognitive, 89, 91–93
    positive, 167
relationships
    boundaries in, 76
    debate as eroding, 152–154
    disagreement as straining, 49
    granting airtime in, 45–46
    honesty vs. peacekeeping in,
        24–25
    vs. illusion of asymmetric
        insight, 135–136
    power dynamics in, 39–41
    practicing respectful dissent
        in, 183
    strengthening, 125
representation, 138–141
resources, 197, 206
respect
    about shared perspectives, 177
    agreeing to, 71, 209
    amidst difference, 24–25, 169
    as beyond agreement, 42
    boundaries for, 75
    culture and, 41–42
    in dialogue, 156–157
    from disrespect to, 29–30
    in the face of hate, 162–163
    as a gift, 39
    via humanization, 3–4, 46
    in meetings, 203
    personality and, 46
    as recognition of worth, 11
"Respect" song, 35–36
respectful disagreement
    boundaries in, 75–77
    choice of medium for,
        174–176
    as collaborative, 149
    vs. dehumanization, 3
    dialogue for, 155–157
    forgiveness and, 55
    how to, 30, 165, 198–200
    intentional exposure to, 96
    politeness is not, 42–43
    time and place for, 62–64, 165
responsibility, 40–41
Robilotta, James, 122

S

safety
    boundaries for, 80–81
    emotional, 75, 80–81
    for engaging disagreements,
        165
selective exposure, 95–97
self
    3Self Model, 105–109
    check-ins with, 165, 198
    cognitive reframing and,
        91–93
    humanization and, 103
    maintaining balance in, 108
    reflection of potential, 163
self-awareness, 198
self-care, 62–64
self-talk, positive, 89, 200
sexuality, 101
sharing, 176–178, 183
silence, 41–42, 62–63
simplification, 141
small sample size, 138–141

society
    dehumanization/humanization
        in, 103–104
    respect norms in, 37–38
softening words, 167
South Africa, 67–68
spoken communication, 175, 176
statements, making, 198
status quo, challenging, 42–43
stereotyping, 145–146
strategic action, 10
stress, 198
student, being a, 117–118
Superior Self, 106–108, 177
superiority
    cognitive reframing and,
        92–93
    dehumanization via, 101
    effect on actions, 59
    and illusion of asymmetric
        insight, 135–136
    and personality disorders, 102
suppression of disagreement, 25

T
TEDx talk, 197
"tell me more," 134, 199
texting, 175
"Thank You, Because," 161,
    172–173, 199
3FA model, 161, 170–172, 199
3Self Model, 13, 105–109
tone of voice, 170, 174
Tortoise Principle, 9–10, 183
transformation, 161, 163
trauma, 53–56
trust
    betrayal of, 22
    boundaries and, 76, 81
    disagreement amidst, 81, 89
    fostering, 125
    via honest dialogue, 156
    power imbalance vs., 40
    productive disagreements
        via, 165

with verification, 206
of a younger generation, 34

U
uncertainty, embracing, 167
understanding
    boundaries for, 76
    as a bridge, 69
    broadening, 146
    cognitive reframing for, 94
    conversational receptiveness
        for, 110
    cultivating, 50
    via curiosity, 136, 137
    vs. debate, 154
    via dialogue, 155
    of high-commitment
        beliefs, 98
    large sample size for, 141
    via listening fully, 123
    need for, 4
    our personal history, 53–56
    patience and, 81
    respectful disagreement via,
        200
    search for, 123–126
United Nations, 2

V
values, personal, 47
verbal attacks, 43, 56, 79
verification, 206
violence
    difference of opinion and, 2–3
    violent conflict statistics, 2–3
visual cues, 175
voice, 164, 174
voicing ideas, 157, 175
vulnerability, 81, 165, 201

W
walking, 203, 205
"why," finding our, 26
women, 101
word choice, 174

Work. Meaningful., 7, 119, 197
workplace
    boundaries in, 77–78
    cultural impacts in, 168–170
    navigating issues in, 4
    power dynamics in, 43–45
    resources, 197
    silence in, 62–63
written communication, 175, 176

Y

Yerkes-Dodson law, 118–119
"you" statements, 167

Z

zero-sum scenarios, 171
Zhao, Xuan, 172, 173

ABOUT THE AUTHOR

Justin Jones-Fosu: Bridging Work and Purpose

Dedicated husband, doting father, and social entrepreneur Justin Jones-Fosu stands at the nexus of purpose-driven work and living. Beyond his responsibilities at home—whether it's tackling the laundry or other family "projects"—he is a global force, delivering forty to fifty presentations yearly to leading corporations, associations, and educational institutions.

For over twenty years, Justin's fervent pursuit has been crystal clear: to champion the intrinsic worth of every individual. This conviction anchors his prolific career blending research with dynamic speaking, writing, and consulting. By doing so, he empowers organizations to nurture meaningful workplaces and helps individuals infuse purpose into their homes and communities. Born out of countless presentations and rich experiences, his books are a testament to his audience's hunger for more.

But what sparked this journey? As a curious child, Justin might have tested his mother's patience with his relentless *whys*, but they also nurtured his inquisitive spirit. Label-defying from the start, he was the athletic nerd who immersed himself in John Grisham novels and confidently sported suits and carried a briefcase to school. These unique intersections taught Justin the priceless skill of connecting worlds, serving as a bridge for diverse groups.

This ethos led him to the realm of human resources, focusing on corporate training and development, and drove him to acquire his MBA in leadership and organizational learning. Justin is a recipient of multiple accolades for his unwavering commitment to people and purposeful workplaces. His adventures aren't limited to the corporate sphere, either: his treks across iconic landscapes like Mount Kilimanjaro and Machu Picchu symbolize his quest to bridge global divides.

Today, as the founder and CEO of Work. Meaningful., he dedicates himself to transforming workplaces into hubs of meaning and belonging. His influential books, *The Inclusive Mindset* and *Your WHY Matters Now*, underscore his position as a thought leader on inclusion and meaningful work. The Work. Meaningful. team currently conducts keynotes, workshops, training, courses, and consulting for organizations around the globe.

Yet his passion doesn't stop there. As chairperson of the board of the Work. Meaningful. Foundation, he champions educational initiatives in Africa and the United States, from providing essential amenities to constructing school buildings in Ghana.

But if you ask him about his most cherished role? It's being a devoted husband and father to his four vibrant children. For Justin, family eclipses all awards and accomplishments. Residing in Charlotte, North Carolina, and frequently traveling to his cherished Ghana, Justin continues to inspire countless souls. Dive deeper into his mission at *WorkMeaningful .com* and *WorkMeaningfulFoundation.org*.

SHARE YOUR THOUGHTS

The biggest thank you one can give is leaving an honest review. It is also the best way for others to learn and share the *I Respectfully Disagree* message with others. Please consider going to wherever you purchased this book and sharing your perspective. Thank you for helping me spread this humanizing message.

You are appreciated!!! Thank you in advance. Also, if you would like to share how this book impacted you, email us directly at *engage@workmeaningful.com*

Berrett–Koehler
Publishers

Berrett-Koehler is an independent publisher dedicated to an ambitious mission: *Connecting people and ideas to create a world that works for all.*

Our publications span many formats, including print, digital, audio, and video. We also offer online resources, training, and gatherings. And we will continue expanding our products and services to advance our mission.

We believe that the solutions to the world's problems will come from all of us, working at all levels: in our society, in our organizations, and in our own lives. Our publications and resources offer pathways to creating a more just, equitable, and sustainable society. They help people make their organizations more humane, democratic, diverse, and effective (and we don't think there's any contradiction there). And they guide people in creating positive change in their own lives and aligning their personal practices with their aspirations for a better world.

And we strive to practice what we preach through what we call "The BK Way." At the core of this approach is *stewardship,* a deep sense of responsibility to administer the company for the benefit of all of our stakeholder groups, including authors, customers, employees, investors, service providers, sales partners, and the communities and environment around us. Everything we do is built around stewardship and our other core values of *quality, partnership, inclusion,* and *sustainability.*

This is why Berrett-Koehler is the first book publishing company to be both a B Corporation (a rigorous certification) and a benefit corporation (a for-profit legal status), which together require us to adhere to the highest standards for corporate, social, and environmental performance. And it is why we have instituted many pioneering practices (which you can learn about at www.bkconnection.com), including the Berrett-Koehler Constitution, the Bill of Rights and Responsibilities for BK Authors, and our unique Author Days.

We are grateful to our readers, authors, and other friends who are supporting our mission. We ask you to share with us examples of how BK publications and resources are making a difference in your lives, organizations, and communities at www.bkconnection.com/impact.

Dear reader,

Thank you for picking up this book and welcome to the worldwide BK community! You're joining a special group of people who have come together to create positive change in their lives, organizations, and communities.

What's BK all about?

Our mission is to connect people and ideas to create a world that works for all.

Why? Our communities, organizations, and lives get bogged down by old paradigms of self-interest, exclusion, hierarchy, and privilege. But we believe that can change. That's why we seek the leading experts on these challenges—and share their actionable ideas with you.

A welcome gift

To help you get started, we'd like to offer you a **free copy** of one of our bestselling ebooks:

www.bkconnection.com/welcome

When you claim your **free ebook**, you'll also be subscribed to our blog.

Our freshest insights

Access the best new tools and ideas for leaders at all levels on our blog at ideas.bkconnection.com.

Sincerely,

Your friends at Berrett-Koehler

Certified

Corporation